Balfour Stewart

The conservation of energy being an elementary treatise on energy and its laws

Balfour Stewart
The conservation of energy being an elementary treatise on energy and its laws
ISBN/EAN: 9783742814012

Manufactured in Europe, USA, Canada, Australia, Japa

Cover: Foto ©ninafisch / pixelio.de

Manufactured and distributed by brebook publishing software (www.brebook.com)

Balfour Stewart

The conservation of energy being an elementary treatise on energy and its laws

THE INTERNATIONAL SCIENTIFIC SERIES.

THE VOLUMES ALREADY PUBLISHED ARE:—

THE FORMS OF WATER IN RAIN AND RIVERS, ICE AND GLACIERS. By J. TYNDALL, LL.D., F.R.S. With 26 Illustrations. Crown 8vo. 5s. Third Edition.

"One of Professor Tyndall's best scientific treatises."—*Standard.*
"With the clearness and brilliancy of language which have won for him his fame, he considers the subject of ice, snow, and glaciers."—*Morning Post.*
"Before starting for Switzerland next summer every one should study 'The Forms of Water.'"—*Globe.*
"Eloquent and instructive in an eminent degree."—*British Quarterly.*

PHYSICS AND POLITICS; or, THOUGHTS ON THE APPLICATION OF THE PRINCIPLES OF "NATURAL SELECTION" AND "INHERITANCE" TO POLITICAL SOCIETY. By WALTER BAGEHOT. Crown 8vo. 4s. Second Edition.

"We can recommend the book as well deserving to be read by thoughtful students of politics."—*Saturday Review.*
"Able and ingenious."—*Spectator.*
"A work of really original and interesting speculation. Mr. Bagehot has undertaken to inquire what are the conditions which enable nations to enter on a course of progress, and to continue in it."—*Guardian.*

FOODS. By Dr. EDWARD SMITH. Profusely Illustrated. Price 5s. Second Edition.

"A comprehensive résumé of our present chemical and physiological knowledge of the various foods, solid and liquid, which go so far to ameliorate the troubles and vexations of this anxious and wearying existence."—*Chemist and Druggist.*
"Treats of all animal and vegetable products which are used as food, as to their chemical properties, their physiological effects, and the various modes of their preparation. Every page teems with information."—*Church Herald.*

MIND AND BODY: THE THEORIES OF THEIR RELATIONS. By ALEXANDER BAIN, LL.D., Professor of Logic at the University of Aberdeen. Four Illustrations. 4s. Second Edition.

THE STUDY OF SOCIOLOGY. By HERBERT SPENCER. Price 5s. Second Edition.

ON THE CONSERVATION OF ENERGY. By Professor BALFOUR STEWART. Fourteen Engravings. Price 5s.

Animal Mechanics; or, Walking, Swimming, and Flying. By Dr. J. B. PETTIGREW, M.D. F.R.S. Crown 8vo. 122 Illustrations. 5s.

RESPONSIBILITY IN MENTAL DISEASE. By Dr. HENRY MAUDSLEY.

THE ANIMAL FRAME. By Prof. E. J. MAREY. Crown 8vo. 119 Illustrations. 5s.

☞ For List of Authors, and the Subjects of their forthcoming Books, see end of the book.

HENRY S. KING & Co. 65 CORNHILL, and 12 PATERNOSTER ROW.

THE INTERNATIONAL SCIENTIFIC SERIES

THE
CONSERVATION OF ENERGY

BEING AN ELEMENTARY TREATISE

ON ENERGY AND ITS LAWS

BY

BALFOUR STEWART, M.A. LL.D. F.R.S.

PROFESSOR OF NATURAL PHILOSOPHY AT THE OWENS COLLEGE, MANCHESTER

WITH FOURTEEN ILLUSTRATIONS

SECOND EDITION

HENRY S. KING & CO.
65 CORNHILL, & 12 PATERNOSTER ROW, LONDON
1874

(*The rights of translation and reproduction are reserved.*)

PREFACE.

We may regard the Universe in the light of a vast physical machine, and our knowledge of it may be conveniently divided into two branches.

The one of these embraces what we know regarding the structure of the machine itself, and the other what we know regarding its method of working.

It has appeared to the author that, in a treatise like this, these two branches of knowledge ought as much as possible to be studied together, and he has therefore endeavoured to adopt this course in the following pages. He has regarded a universe composed of atoms with some sort of medium between them as the machine, and the laws of energy as the laws of working of this machine.

The first chapter embraces what we know regarding atoms, and gives also a definition of Energy. The various forces and energies of nature are thereafter enumerated, and the law of Conservation is stated. Then follow the various transmutations of Energy, according to a list, for which the author is indebted to Prof. Tait. The fifth chapter gives a short historical sketch of the subject, ending with the law of Dissipation; while the sixth and last chapter gives some account of the position of living beings in this universe of Energy.

The Owens College, Manchester,
    August, 1873.

TABLE OF CONTENTS.

CHAPTER I.

WHAT IS ENERGY?

	ARTICLE	PAGE
Our Ignorance of Individuals	1—4	1
In the Organic World	5, 6	3
In the Inorganic World	7—9	5
Activity of Molecules	10, 11	7
Action and Reaction, Equal and Opposite.		
Illustrated by a Vessel of Goldfish	12	8
" by a Rifle	13, 14	9
" by a Falling Stone	15, 16	11
The Rifle further considered	17	12
The Rifle Ball possesses Energy	18	13
Definition of Energy	19	13
Energy is proportional to Mass	20	14
It is not simply proportional to Velocity	21, 22	14
Definition of Work	23	15
Rule for measuring Work	24	16

TABLE OF CONTENTS.

	ARTICLE	PAGE
Relation between Velocity and Energy.		
Definition of Velocity	25	16
Kilogramme Weight shot upwards	26, 27	17
Energy proportional to Square of Velocity	28	19
Examples	29	20
Resistance and Buoyancy of Atmosphere Disregarded	30	20
Energy independent of Direction of Motion	31	21
Other Forces besides Gravity	32, 33	21

CHAPTER II.

MECHANICAL ENERGY AND ITS CHANGE INTO HEAT.

	ARTICLE	PAGE
Energy of Position.		
A Stone high up	34	23
A Head of Water	35	24
A Cross-bow bent—a Watch wound up	36	25
Advantage of Position	37	26
Transmutations of Visible Energy.		
A Kilogramme shot upwards	38	27
A Kilogramme descending	39	28
Velocity in the Inclined Plane	40, 41	28
Functions of a Machine.		
A Machine merely transmutes Energy	42	30
This Illustrated by a Set of Pulleys	42	30
" by a Hydrostatic Press	43	32
Principle of Virtual Velocities (What we gain in power we lose in space).		
First clearly defined by Galileo	44	33

	ARTICLE	PAGE
Illustrated by a Lever	44	34
" by an Inclined Plane	45	34

What Friction and Percussion do.

	ARTICLE	PAGE
Friction converts Energy into a less useful Form	46	35
Percussion does the same	47	36
When Friction and Percussion destroy Motion, Heat appears	48	37

Heat a species of Motion.

	ARTICLE	PAGE
Davy's Experiments	49—51	38
Rumford's Experiments	52	39
Argument derived from these	53—55	39

Heat a Backward and Forward Motion.

	ARTICLE	PAGE
A Heated Substance not in Motion as a whole	56	41
Analogy between Heat and Sound	57	42

Mechanical Equivalent of Heat.

	ARTICLE	PAGE
Heating Effects proportional to Energy	58	43
Joule's Experiments	59—61	44
Value of Heat unit	62	46
There are other Varieties of Energy	63	47

CHAPTER III.

THE FORCES AND ENERGIES OF NATURE: THE LAW OF CONSERVATION.

	ARTICLE	PAGE
Connexion between the Energies and Forces of Nature	64	48

Forces of Nature enumerated.

	ARTICLE	PAGE
(1) Gravitation; Its Law of Action	65	48

TABLE OF CONTENTS.

	ARTICLE	PAGE
Gravitation is a Weak Force	66	50
(2) Elastic Forces	67	50
(3) Force of Cohesion (Molecules and Atoms defined)	68, 69	51
(4) Force of Chemical Affinity	70, 71	53
Remarks on Molecular and Atomic Forces	72—78	55

Electricity: its Properties.

	ARTICLE	PAGE
Remarks on Electricity	79, 80	60
Conductors and Non-Conductors	80	61
Two kinds of Electricity	81	62
These two kinds always developed together	82	63
Electrical Hypothesis	83	63
Electricity is only produced when Heterogeneous Bodies are rubbed	84	64
Electricity is probably allied to Chemical Affinity	84	64
List of Substances which develop Electricity	85	64
Electric Machine	86	65
Electric Induction	87, 88	65
Leyden Jar	89, 90	67
The Electric Current described	91, 92	69
The Poles of a Battery	92	71
The Electrical Condition of the Poles	93	71
Direction of Battery Current	94, 95	71
Magnetic Effects of Current	96, 97	72
Heating Effect of Current	98	73
Chemical Effect of Current	99	74
Attraction and Repulsion of Currents	100	74

TABLE OF CONTENTS.   xi

	ARTICLE	PAGE
Attraction and Repulsion of Magnets	101	75
Induction of Currents	102—105	75

Energies of Nature enumerated.

(A) Energy of Visible Motion	107	78
(B) Visible Energy of Position	108, 109	79
(C) Heat Motion	110	80
(D) Molecular Separation	110	80
(E) Atomic or Chemical Separation	111	80
(F) Electrical Separation	112	81
(G) Electricity in Motion	113	81
(H) Radiant Energy	114	81

Law of Conservation.

| Statement of Law | 115, 116 | 82 |
| Nature of Proof of Law | 117—120 | 83 |

CHAPTER IV.

TRANSMUTATIONS OF ENERGY.

Energy of Visible Motion.

(1) Into Energy of Position	121, 122	87
(2) Into Absorbed Heat in Motions on the Earth	123—131	89
Into Absorbed Heat in Planetary Motions	132—137	93
(3) Into Electrical Separation (Electric Machine)	138, 139	98
(4) Into a Current of Electricity	140—143	99
Magneto-Electricity	144—147	103

	ARTICLE	PAGE

Visible Energy of Position.
 Into Energy of Visible Motion .   148 ... 105

Absorbed Heat in its two Forms.
 (1) Into Energy of Visible Motion in the Heat Engine .   149 ... 105
  Law of Working of Heat Engines   150—152 ... 106
  An Ordinary Fire .   153 ... 106
  The Earth an Engine .   154 ... 106
  Remarks on Engines .   155 ... 109
  Pressure lowers Freezing Point of Water .   156 ... 110
 (2) The one Form into the Other—in Change of State .   157 ... 112
  Prince Rupert's Drops .   158 ... 114
 (3) Into Chemical Separation .   159 ... 114
  Temperature of Disassociation .   159 ... 115
 (4) Into Electrical Separation, when Tourmalines, &c., are heated .   160 ... 115
 (5) Into Electricity in motion—in Thermo-Electricity .   161 ... 116
 (6) Into Radiant Light and Heat .   162 ... 117
  Analogy between a Hot and a Sounding Body .   162 ... 118

Chemical Separation.
 (1) Into Heat, when Bodies are Burned .   163, 164 ... 118
  Metallic Precipitates .   165, 166 ... 120
  Change of Condition accompanies Chemical Action .   167 ... 121

	ARTICLE	PAGE
(2) Into Electrical Separation, when Heterogeneous Metals are Soldered together	168	122
(3) Into Electricity in Motion—in the Voltaic Battery	169, 170	123

Electrical Separation.

(1) Into Visible Motion	171	124
(2) Into a Current of Electricity	172	124

Electricity in Motion.

(1) Into Visible Motion (Attraction of Currents)	173	124
(2) Into Heat (In a Resisting Body)	174, 175	125
Peltier's Experiment	176	126
(3) Into Chemical Separation—in Decomposition by the Battery	177	127

Radiant Energy.

(1) Into Absorbed Heat	178	128
(2) Into Chemical Separation (in the Leaves of Plants, &c.)	179, 181	128

CHAPTER V.

HISTORICAL SKETCH: THE DISSIPATION OF ENERGY.

Problems allied to Energy	182, 183	131
Heraclitus on Energy	184	133
Democritus on Atoms	185	133
Bacon's Remarks	185	134

TABLE OF CONTENTS.

	ARTICLE	PAGE
Aristotle on a Medium	185	134
Whewell's Remarks	186	134
The Ideas of the Ancients not Prolific	187, 188	135
Descartes, Newton, and Huyghens on a Medium	189	136
Bacon on Heat	190	137
Principle of Virtual Velocities	191	137
Rise of True Conceptions regarding Work	192	138
Perpetual Motion	193	139
Theory of Conservation	194	140
Dissipation of Energy	195	141
Natural Energies and their Sources	196	143
(1) Fuel, embracing Wood and Coal	197	143
(2) Food	199	145
(3) Head of Water	200	146
(4) Tidal Energy	201	146
(5) Native Sulphur, &c.	202	147
(6) Air and Water in Motion	203	147
These come chiefly from the Sun	203	147
The Sun—a Source of High Temperature Heat	204	148
A Perpetual Light Impossible	205	149
The Sun is no Exception	206	150
Origin of the Sun's Heat	207—209	150
Probable Fate of the Universe	209—210	152

CHAPTER VI.

THE POSITION OF LIFE.

	ARTICLE	PAGE
Preliminary Remarks	211	154
Twofold Nature of Equilibrium	212	154
Mechanical Instability	213, 214	155
Chemical Instability	215	156
Machines are of Two Kinds	216—220	157
An Animal is a Delicately-constructed Machine	221	160
Life is like the Commander of an Army	222—226	171
Organized Tissues are Subject to Decay	227, 228	164
Difference between Animals and Inanimate Machines	229	165
Ultimate Dependence of Life upon the Sun	230—232	165

THE CONSERVATION OF ENERGY.

CHAPTER I.

WHAT IS ENERGY?

Our Ignorance of Individuals.

1. VERY often we know little or nothing of individuals, while we yet possess a definite knowledge of the laws which regulate communities.

The Registrar-General, for example, will tell us that the death-rate in London varies with the temperature in such a manner that a very low temperature is invariably accompanied by a very high death-rate. But if we ask him to select some one individual, and explain to us in what manner his death was caused by the low temperature, he will, most probably, be unable to do so.

Again, we may be quite sure that after a bad harvest there will be a large importation of wheat into the country, while, at the same time, we are quite ignorant of the individual journeys of the various particles of flour that go to make up a loaf of bread.

Or yet again, we know that there is a constant carriage of air from the poles to the equator, as shown by the trade winds, and yet no man is able to individualize a particle of this air, and describe its various motions.

2. Nor is our knowledge of individuals greater in the domains of physical science. We know nothing, or next to nothing, of the ultimate structure and properties of matter, whether organic or inorganic.

No doubt there are certain cases where a large number of particles are linked together, so as to act as one individual, and then we can predict its action—as, for instance, in the solar system, where the physical astronomer is able to foretell with great exactness the positions of the various planets, or of the moon. And so, in human affairs, we find a large number of individuals acting together as one nation, and the sagacious statesman taking very much the place of the sagacious astronomer, with regard to the action and reaction of various nations upon one another.

But if we ask the astronomer or the statesman to select an individual particle and an individual human being, and predict the motions of each, we shall find that both will be completely at fault.

3. Nor have we far to look for the cause of their ignorance. A continuous and restless, nay, a very complicated, activity is the order of nature throughout all her indi-

viduals, whether these be living beings or inanimate particles of matter. Existence is, in truth, one continued fight, and a great battle is always and everywhere raging, although the field in which it is fought is often completely shrouded from our view.

4. Nevertheless, although we cannot trace the motions of individuals, we may sometimes tell the result of the fight, and even predict how the day will go, as well as specify the causes that contribute to bring about the issue.

With great freedom of action and much complication of motion in the individual, there are yet comparatively simple laws regulating the joint result attainable by the community.

But, before proceeding to these, it may not be out of place to take a very brief survey of the organic and inorganic worlds, in order that our readers, as well as ourselves, may realize our common ignorance of the ultimate structure and properties of matter.

5. Let us begin by referring to the causes which bring about disease. It is only very recently that we have begun to suspect a large number of our diseases to be caused by organic germs. Now, assuming that we are right in this, it must nevertheless be confessed that our ignorance about these germs is most complete. It is perhaps doubtful whether we ever saw one of these organisms,*

* It is said that there are one or two instances where the microscope has enlarged them into visibility.

while it is certain that we are in profound ignorance of their properties and habits.

We are told by some writers * that the very air we breathe is absolutely teeming with germs, and that we are surrounded on all sides by an innumerable army of minute organic beings. It has also been conjectured that they are at incessant warfare among themselves, and that we form the spoil of the stronger party. Be this as it may, we are at any rate intimately bound up with, and, so to speak, at the mercy of, a world of creatures, of which we know as little as of the inhabitants of the planet Mars.

6. Yet, even here, with profound ignorance of the individual, we are not altogether unacquainted with some of the habits of these powerful predatory communities. Thus we know that cholera is eminently a low level disease, and that during its ravages we ought to pay particular attention to the water we drink. This is a general law of cholera, which is of the more importance to us because we cannot study the habits of the individual organisms that cause the disease.

Could we but see these, and experiment upon them, we should soon acquire a much more extensive knowledge of their habits, and perhaps find out the means of extirpating the disease, and of preventing its recurrence.

Again, we know (thanks to Jenner) that vaccination will prevent the ravages of small-pox, but in this in-

* See Dr. Angus Smith on Air and Rain.

stance we are no better off than a band of captives who have found out in what manner to mutilate themselves, so as to render them uninteresting to their victorious foe.

7. But if our knowledge of the nature and habits of organized molecules be so small, our knowledge of the ultimate molecules of inorganic matter is, if possible, still smaller. It is only very recently that the leading men of science have come to consider their very existence as a settled point.

In order to realize what is meant by an inorganic molecule, let us take some sand and grind it into smaller and smaller particles, and these again into still smaller. In point of fact we shall never reach the superlative degree of smallness by this operation—yet in our imagination we may suppose the sub-division to be carried on continuously, always making the particles smaller and smaller. In this case we should, at last, come to an ultimate molecule of sand or oxide of silicon, or, in other words, we should arrive at the smallest entity retaining all the properties of sand, so that were it possible to divide the molecule further the only result would be to separate it into its chemical constituents, consisting of silicon on the one side and oxygen on the other.

We have, in truth, much reason to believe that sand, or any other substance, is incapable of infinite sub-division, and that all we can do in grinding down a solid lump of anything is to reduce it into lumps similar to the original, but only less in size, each of these small lumps containing probably a great number of individual molecules.

8. Now, a drop of water no less than a grain of sand is built up of a very great number of molecules, attached to one another by the force of cohesion—a force which is much stronger in the sand than in the water, but which nevertheless exists in both. And, moreover, Sir William Thomson, the distinguished physicist, has recently arrived at the following conclusion with regard to the size of the molecules of water. He imagines a single drop of water to be magnified until it becomes as large as the earth, having a diameter of 8000 miles, and all the molecules to be magnified in the same proportion; and he then concludes that a single molecule will appear, under these circumstances, as somewhat larger than a shot, and somewhat smaller than a cricket ball.

9. Whatever be the value of this conclusion, it enables us to realize the exceedingly small size of the individual molecules of matter, and renders it quite certain that we shall never, by means of the most powerful microscope, succeed in making visible these ultimate molecules. For our knowledge of the sizes, shapes, and properties of such bodies, we must always, therefore, be indebted to indirect evidence of a very complicated nature.

It thus appears that we know little or nothing about the shape or size of molecules, or about the forces which actuate them; and, moreover, the very largest masses of the universe share with the very smallest this property

of being beyond the direct scrutiny of the human senses
—the one set because they are so far away, and the other
because they are so small.

10. Again, these molecules are not at rest, but, on the contrary, they display an intense and ceaseless energy in their motions. There is, indeed, an uninterrupted warfare going on—a constant clashing together of these minute bodies, which are continually maimed, and yet always recover themselves, until, perhaps, some blow is struck sufficiently powerful to dissever the two or more simple atoms that go to form a compound molecule. A new state of things thenceforward is the result.

But a simple elementary atom is truly an immortal being, and enjoys the privilege of remaining unaltered and essentially unaffected amid the most powerful blows that can be dealt against it—it is probably in a state of ceaseless activity and change of form, but it is nevertheless always the same.

11. Now, a little reflection will convince us that we have in this ceaseless activity another barrier to an intimate acquaintance with molecules and atoms, for even if we could see them they would not remain at rest sufficiently long to enable us to scrutinize them.

No doubt there are devices by means of which we can render visible, for instance, the pattern of a quickly revolving coloured disc, for we may illuminate it by a flash of electricity, and the disc may be supposed to be stationary during the extremely short time of the flash.

But we cannot say the same about molecules and atoms, for, could we see an atom, and could we illuminate it by a flash of electricity, the atom would most probably have vibrated many times during the exceedingly small time of the flash. In fine, the limits placed upon our senses, with respect to space and time, equally preclude the possibility of our ever becoming directly acquainted with these exceedingly minute bodies, which are nevertheless the raw materials of which the whole universe is built.

Action and Reaction, Equal and Opposite.

12. But while an impenetrable veil is drawn over the individual in this warfare of clashing atoms, yet we are not left in profound ignorance of the laws which determine the ultimate result of all these motions, taken together as a whole.

In a Vessel of Goldfish.

Let us suppose, for instance, that we have a glass globe containing numerous goldfish standing on the table, and delicately poised on wheels, so that the slightest push, the one way or the other, would make it move. These goldfish are in active and irregular motion, and he would be a very bold man who should venture to predict the movements of an individual fish. But of one thing we may be quite certain: we may rest assured that, notwithstanding all the irregular motions of its living inhabitants, the globe containing the goldfish will remain at rest upon its wheels.

Even if the table were a lake of ice, and the wheels were extremely delicate, we should find that the globe would remain at rest. Indeed, we should be exceedingly surprised if we found the globe going away of its own accord from the one side of the table to the other, or from the one side of a sheet of ice to the other, in consequence of the internal motions of its inhabitants. Whatever be the motions of these individual units, yet we feel sure that the globe cannot move itself *as a whole*. In such a system, therefore, and, indeed, in every system left to itself, there may be strong internal forces acting between the various parts, but these *actions and reactions are equal and opposite*, so that while the small parts, whether visible or invisible, are in violent commotion among themselves, yet the system as a whole will remain at rest.

In a Rifle.

13. Now it is quite a legitimate step to pass from this instance of the goldfish to that of a rifle that has just been fired. In the former case, we imagined the globe, together with its fishes, to form one system; and in the latter, we must look upon the rifle, with its powder and ball, as forming one system also.

Let us suppose that the explosion takes place through the application of a spark. Although this spark is an external agent, yet if we reflect a little we shall see that its only office in this case is to summon up the internal forces already existing in the loaded rifle, and bring them into vigorous action, and that in virtue of these internal forces the explosion takes place.

The most prominent result of this explosion is the out-rush of the rifle ball with a velocity that may, perhaps, carry it for the best part of a mile before it comes to rest; and here it would seem to us, at first sight, that the law of equal action and reaction is certainly broken, for these internal forces present in the rifle have at least propelled part of the system, namely, the rifle ball, with a most enormous velocity in one direction.

14. But a little further reflection will bring to light another phenomenon besides the out-rush of the ball. It is well known to all sportsmen that when a fowling-piece is discharged, there is a kick or recoil of the piece itself against the shoulder of the sportsman, which he would rather get rid of, but which we most gladly welcome as the solution of our difficulty. In plain terms, while the ball is projected forwards, the rifle stock (if free to move) is at the same moment projected backwards. To fix our ideas, let us suppose that the rifle stock weighs 100 ounces, and the ball one ounce, and that the ball is projected forwards with the velocity of 1000 feet per second; then it is asserted, by the law of action and reaction, that the rifle stock is at the same time projected backwards with the velocity of 10 feet per second, so that the mass of the stock, multiplied by its velocity of

recoil, shall precisely equal the mass of the ball, multiplied by its velocity of projection. The one product forms a measure of the action in the one direction, and the other of the reaction in the opposite direction, and thus we see that in the case of a rifle, as well as in that of the globe of fish, action and reaction are equal and opposite.

In a Falling Stone.

15. We may even extend the law to cases in which we do not perceive the recoil or reaction at all. Thus, if I drop a stone from the top of a precipice to the earth, the motion seems all to be in one direction, while at the same time it is in truth the result of a mutual attraction between the earth and the stone. Does not the earth move also? We cannot see it move, but we are entitled to assert that it does in reality move upwards to meet the stone, although quite to an imperceptible extent, and that the law of action and reaction holds here as truly as in a rifle, the only difference being that in the one case the two objects are rushing together, while in the other they are rushing apart. Inasmuch, however, as the mass of the earth is very great compared with that of the stone, it follows that its velocity must be extremely small, in order that the mass of the earth, multiplied into its velocity upwards, shall equal the mass of the stone, multiplied into its velocity downwards.

16. We have thus, in spite of our ignorance of the ultimate atoms and molecules of matter, arrived at a

general law which regulates the action of internal forces. We see that these forces are always mutually exerted, and that if A attracts or repels B, B in its turn attracts or repels A. We have here, in fact, a very good instance of that kind of generalization, which we may arrive at, even in spite of our ignorance of individuals.

But having now arrived at this law of action and reaction, do we know all that it is desirable to know? have we got a complete understanding of what takes place in all such cases—for instance, in that of the rifle which is just discharged? Let us consider this point a little further.

The Rifle further considered.

17. We define quantity of motion to mean the product of the mass by the velocity; and since the velocity of recoil of the rifle stock, multiplied by the mass of the stock, is equal to the velocity of projection of the rifle ball, multiplied by the mass of the ball, we conceive ourselves entitled to say that the quantity of motion, or momentum, generated is equal in both directions, so that the law of action and reaction holds here also. Nevertheless, it cannot but occur to us that, *in some sense*, the motion of the rifle ball is a very different thing from that of the stock, for it is one thing to allow the stock to recoil against your shoulder and discharge the ball into the air, and a very different thing to discharge the ball against your shoulder and allow the stock to fly into the

air. And if any man should assert the absolute equality between the blow of the rifle stock and that of the rifle ball, you might request him to put his assertion to this practical test, with the absolute certainty that he would decline. Equality between the two!—Impossible! Why, if this were the case, a company of soldiers engaged in war would suffer much more than the enemy against whom they fired, for the soldiers would certainly feel each recoil, while the enemy would suffer from only a small proportion of the bullets.

The Rifle Ball possesses Energy.

18. Now, what is the meaning of this great difference between the two? We have a vivid perception of a mighty difference, and it only remains for us to clothe our naked impressions in a properly fitting scientific garb.

The something which the rifle ball possesses in contradistinction to the rifle stock is clearly the power of overcoming resistance. It can penetrate through oak wood or through water, or (alas! that it should be so often tried) through the human body, and this power of penetration is the distinguishing characteristic of a substance moving with very great velocity.

19. Let us define by the term *energy* this power which the rifle ball possesses of overcoming obstacles or of doing work. Of course we use the word work without reference to the moral character of the thing done, and con-

ceive ourselves entitled to sum up, with perfect propriety and innocence, the amount of work done in drilling a hole through a deal board or through a man.

20. A body such as a rifle ball, moving with very great velocity, has, therefore, energy, and it requires very little consideration to perceive that this *energy will be proportional to its weight or mass*, for a ball of two ounces moving with the velocity of 1000 feet per second will be the same as two balls of one ounce moving with this velocity, but the energy of two similarly moving ounce balls will manifestly be double that of one, so that the energy is proportional to the weight, if we imagine that, meanwhile, the velocity remains the same.

21. But, on the other hand, the energy is not simply proportional to the velocity, for, if it were, the energy of the rifle stock and of the rifle ball would be the same, inasmuch as the rifle stock would gain as much by its superior mass as it would lose by its inferior velocity. Therefore, the energy of a moving body increases with the velocity more quickly than a simple proportion, so that if the velocity be doubled, the energy is more than doubled. Now, in what manner does the energy increase with the velocity? That is the question we have now to answer, and, in doing so, we must appeal to the familiar facts of everyday observation and experience.

22. In the first place, it is well known to artillerymen, that if a ball have a double velocity, its penetrating power or energy is increased nearly fourfold, so that it

will pierce through four, or nearly four, times as many deal boards as the ball with only a single velocity—in other words, they will tell us, in mathematical language, that the energy varies as the square of the velocity.

Definition of Work.

23. And now, before proceeding further, it will be necessary to tell our readers how to measure work in a strictly scientific manner. We have defined energy to be the power of doing work, and although every one has a general notion of what is meant by work, that notion may not be sufficiently precise for the purpose of this volume. How, then, are we to measure work? Fortunately, we have not far to go for a practical means of doing this. Indeed, there is a force at hand which enables us to accomplish this measurement with the greatest precision, and this force is gravity. Now, the first operation in any kind of numerical estimate is to fix upon our unit or standard. Thus we say a rod is so many inches long, or a road so many miles long. Here an inch and a mile are chosen as our standards. In like manner, we speak of so many seconds, or minutes, or hours, or days, or years, choosing that standard of time or duration which is most convenient for our purpose. So in like manner we must choose our unit of work, but in order to do so we must first of all choose our units of weight and of length, and for these we will take the *kilogramme* and the *metre*, these being the units of the metrical system. The kilo-

gramme corresponds to about 15,432·35 English grains, being rather more than two pounds avoirdupois, and the metre to about 39·371 English inches.

Now, if we raise a kilogramme weight one metre in vertical height, we are conscious of putting forth an effort to do so, and of being resisted in the act by the force of gravity. In other words, we spend energy and do work in the process of raising this weight.

Let us agree to consider the energy spent, or the work done, in this operation as one unit of work, and let us call it the *kilogrammetre*.

24. In the next place, it is very obvious that if we raise the kilogramme two metres in height, we do two units of work—if three metres, three units, and so on.

And again, it is equally obvious that if we raise a weight of two kilogrammes one metre high, we likewise do two units of work, while if we raise it two metres high, we do four units, and so on.

From these examples we are entitled to derive the following rule:—*Multiply the weight raised (in kilogrammes) by the vertical height (in metres) through which it is raised, and the result will be the work done (in kilogrammetres).*

Relation between Velocity and Energy.

25. Having thus laid a numerical foundation for our superstructure, let us next proceed to investigate the relation between velocity and energy. But first let us say a

few words about velocity. This is one of the few cases in which everyday experience will aid, rather than hinder, us in our scientific conception. Indeed, we have constantly before us the example of bodies moving with variable velocities.

Thus a railway train is approaching a station and is just beginning to slacken its pace. When we begin to observe, it is moving at the rate of forty miles an hour. A minute afterwards it is moving at the rate of twenty miles only, and a minute after that it is at rest. For no two consecutive moments has this train continued to move at the same rate, and yet we may say, with perfect propriety, that at such a moment the train was moving, say, at the rate of thirty miles an hour. We mean, of course, that had it continued to move for an hour with the speed which it had when we made the observation, it would have gone over thirty miles. We know that, as a matter of fact, it did not move for two seconds at that rate, but this is of no consequence, and hardly at all interferes with our mental grasp of the problem, so accustomed are we all to cases of variable velocity.

26. Let us now imagine a kilogramme weight to be shot vertically upwards, with a certain initial velocity—let us say, with the velocity of 9·8 metres in one second. Gravity will, of course, act against the weight, and continually diminish its upward speed, just as in the railway train the break was constantly reducing the

velocity. But yet it is very easy to see what is meant by an initial velocity of 9·8 metres per second; it means that if gravity did not interfere, and if the air did not resist, and, in fine, if no external influence of any kind were allowed to act upon the ascending mass, it would be found to move over 9·8 metres in one second.

Now, it is well known to those who have studied the laws of motion, that a body, shot upwards with the velocity of 9·8 metres in one second, will be brought to rest when it has risen 4·9 metres in height. If, therefore, it be a kilogramme, its upward velocity will have enabled it to raise itself 4·9 metres in height against the force of gravity, or, in other words, it will have done 4·9 units of work; and we may imagine it, when at the top of its ascent, and just about to turn, caught in the hand and lodged on the top of a house, instead of being allowed to fall again to the ground. We are, therefore, entitled to say that a kilogramme, shot upwards with the velocity of 9·8 metres per second, has energy equal to 4·9, inasmuch as it can raise itself 4·9 metres in height.

27. Let us next suppose that the velocity with which the kilogramme is shot upwards is that of 19·6 metres per second. It is known to all who have studied dynamics that the kilogramme will now mount not only twice, but four times as high as it did in the last instance—in other words, it will now mount 19·6 metres in height.

Evidently, then, in accordance with our principles of

measurement, the kilogramme has now four times as much energy as it had in the last instance, because it can raise itself four times as high, and therefore do four times as much work, and thus we see that the energy is increased four times by doubling the velocity.

Had the initial velocity been three times that of the first instance, or 29·4 metres per second, it might in like manner be shown that the height attained would have been 44·1 metres, so that by tripling the velocity the energy is increased nine times.

28. We thus see that whether we measure the energy of a moving body by the thickness of the planks through which it can pierce its way, or by the height to which it can raise itself against gravity, the result arrived at is the same. *We find the energy to be proportional to the square of the velocity*, and we may formularize our conclusion as follows:—

Let $v =$ the initial velocity expressed in metres per second, then the energy in kilogrammetres $= \dfrac{v^2}{19\cdot 6}$. Of course, if the body shot upwards weighs two kilogrammes, then everything is doubled, if three kilogrammes, tripled, and so on; so that finally, if we denote by m the mass of the body in kilogrammes, we shall have the energy in kilogrammetres $= \dfrac{m v^2}{19\cdot 6}$. To test the truth of this formula, we have only to apply it to the cases described in Arts. 26 and 27.

29. We may further illustrate it by one or two examples. For instance, let it be required to find the energy contained in a mass of five kilogrammes, shot upwards with the velocity of 20 metres per second.

Here we have $m = 5$ and $v = 20$, hence—

$$\text{Energy} = \frac{5\,(20)^2}{19\cdot 6} = \frac{2000}{19\cdot 6} = 102\cdot 04 \text{ nearly.}$$

Again, let it be required to find the height to which the mass of the last question will ascend before it stops. We know that its energy is $102\cdot 04$, and that its mass is 5. Dividing $102\cdot 04$ by 5, we obtain $20\cdot 408$ as the height to which this mass of five kilogrammes must ascend in order to do work equal to $102\cdot 04$ kilogrammetres.

30. In what we have said we have taken no account either of the resistance or of the buoyancy of the atmosphere; in fact, we have supposed the experiments to be made in vacuo, or, if not in vacuo, made by means of a heavy mass, like lead, which will be very little influenced either by the resistance or buoyancy of the air.

We must not, however, forget that if a sheet of paper, or a feather, be shot upwards with the velocities mentioned in our text, they will certainly not rise in the air to nearly the height recorded, but will be much sooner brought to a stop by the very great resistance which they encounter from the air, on account of their great surface, combined with their small mass.

On the other hand, if the substance we make use of be a large light bag filled with hydrogen, it will find its way upwards without any effort on our part, and we shall certainly be doing no work by carrying it one or more metres in height—it will, in reality, help to pull us up, instead of requiring help from us to cause it to ascend. In fine, what we have said is meant to refer to the force of gravity alone, without taking into account a resisting medium such as the atmosphere, the existence of which need not be considered in our present calculations.

31. It should likewise be remembered, that while the energy of a moving body depends upon its velocity, it is independent of the direction in which the body is moving. We have supposed the body to be shot upwards with a given velocity, but it might be shot horizontally with the same velocity, when it would have precisely the same energy as before. A cannon ball, if fired vertically upwards, may either be made to spend its energy in raising itself, or in piercing through a series of deal boards. Now, if the same ball be fired horizontally with the same velocity it will pierce through the same number of deal boards.

In fine, direction of motion is of no consequence, and the only reason why we have chosen vertical motion is that, in this case, there is always the force of gravity steadily and constantly opposing the motion of the body, and enabling us to obtain an accurate measure of the work which it does by piercing its way upwards against this force.

32. But gravity is not the only force, and we might

measure the energy of a moving body by the extent to which it would bend a powerful spring or resist the attraction of a powerful magnet, or, in fine, we might make use of the force which best suits our purpose. If this force be a constant one, we must measure the energy of the moving body by the space which it is able to traverse against the action of the force—just as, in the case of gravity, we measured the energy of the body by the space through which it was able to raise itself against its own weight.

33. We must, of course, bear in mind that if this force be more powerful than gravity, a body moved a short distance against it will represent the expenditure of as much energy as if it were moved a greater distance against gravity. In fine, we must take account both of the strength of the force and of the distance moved over by the body against it before we can estimate in an accurate matter the work which has been done.

CHAPTER II.

MECHANICAL ENERGY AND ITS CHANGE INTO HEAT.

Energy of Position. A Stone high up.

34. In the last chapter it was shown what is meant by energy, and how it depends upon the velocity of a moving body; and now let us state that this same energy or power of doing work may nevertheless be possessed by a body absolutely at rest. It will be remembered (Art. 26) that in one case where a kilogramme was shot vertically upwards, we supposed it to be caught at the summit of its flight and lodged on the top of a house. Here, then, it rests without motion, but yet not without the power of doing work, and hence not without energy. For we know very well that if we let it fall it will strike the ground with as much velocity, and, therefore, with as much energy, as it had when it was originally projected upwards. Or we may, if we choose, make use of its energy to assist us in driving in a pile, or utilize it in a multitude of ways.

In its lofty position it is, therefore, not without energy, but this is of a quiet nature, and not due in the least to motion. To what, then, is it due? We reply—to the position which the kilogramme occupies at the top of the house. For just as a body in motion is a very different thing (as regards energy) from a body at rest, so is a body at the top of a house a very different thing from a body at the bottom.

To illustrate this, we may suppose that two men of equal activity and strength are fighting together, each having his pile of stones with which he is about to belabour his adversary. One man, however, has secured for himself and his pile an elevated position on the top of a house, while his enemy has to remain content with a position at the bottom. Now, under these circumstances, you can at once tell which of the two will gain the day —evidently the man on the top of the house, and yet not on account of his own superior energy, but rather on account of the energy which he derives from the elevated position of his pile of stones. We thus see that there is a kind of energy derived from position, as well as a kind derived from velocity, and we shall, in future, call the former *energy of position*, and the latter *energy of motion*.

A Head of Water.

35. In order to vary our illustration, let us suppose there are two mills, one with a large pond of water near it and at a high level, while the other has also a pond, but at a lower level than itself. We need hardly ask

MECHANICAL ENERGY AND ITS CHANGE INTO HEAT. 25

which of the two is likely to work—clearly the one with the pond at a low level can derive from it no advantage whatever, while the other may use the high level pond, or head of water, as this is sometimes called, to drive its wheel, and do its work. There is, thus, a great deal of work to be got out of water high up—real substantial work, such as grinding corn or thrashing it, or turning wood or sawing it. On the other hand, there is no work at all to be got from a pond of water that is low down.

A Cross-bow bent. A Watch wound up.

36. In both of the illustrations now given, we have used the force of gravity as that force against which we are to do work, and in virtue of which a stone high up, or a head of water, is in a position of advantage, and has the power of doing work as it falls to a lower level. But there are other forces besides gravity, and, with respect to these, bodies may be in a position of advantage and be able to do work just as truly as the stone, or the head of water, in the case before mentioned.

Let us take, for instance, the force of elasticity, and consider what happens in a cross-bow. When this is bent, the bolt is evidently in a position of advantage with regard to the elastic force of the bow; and when it is discharged, this energy of position of the bolt is converted into energy of motion, just as, when a stone on the top of a house is allowed to fall, its energy of position is converted into that of actual motion.

In like manner a watch wound up is in a position of advantage with respect to the elastic force of the mainspring, and as the wheels of the watch move this is gradually converted into energy of motion

Advantage of Position.

37. It is, in fact, the fate of all kinds of energy of position to be ultimately converted into energy of motion.

The former may be compared to money in a bank, or capital, the latter to money which we are in the act of spending; and just as, when we have money in a bank, we can draw it out whenever we want it, so, in the case of energy of position, we can make use of it whenever we please. To see this more clearly, let us compare together a watermill driven by a head of water, and a windmill driven by the wind. In the one case we may turn on the water whenever it is most convenient for us, but in the other we must wait until the wind happens to blow. The former has all the independence of a rich man; the latter, all the obsequiousness of a poor one. If we pursue the analogy a step further, we shall see that the great capitalist, or the man who has acquired a lofty position, is respected because he has the disposal of a great quantity of energy; and that whether he be a nobleman or a sovereign, or a general in command, he is powerful only from having something which enables him to make use of the services of others. When the man of wealth pays a labouring man to work for him, he is in truth converting so much of his energy of position into actual energy, just as a miller lets out a portion of his head of water in order to do some work by its means.

Transmutations of Visible Energy.—A Kilogramme shot upwards.

38. We have thus endeavoured to show that there is an energy of repose as well as a living energy, an energy of position as well as of motion; and now let us trace the changes which take place in the energy of a weight, shot vertically upwards, as it continues to rise. It starts with a certain amount of energy of motion, but as it ascends, this is by degrees changed into that of position, until, when it gets to the top of its flight, its energy is entirely due to position.

To take an example, let us suppose that a kilogramme is projected vertically upwards with the velocity of 19·6 metres in one second. According to the formula of Art. 28, it contains 19·6 units of energy due to its actual velocity.

If we examine it at the end of one second, we shall find that it has risen 14·7 metres in height, and has now the velocity of 9·8. This velocity we know (Art. 26) denotes an amount of actual energy equal to 4·9, while the height reached corresponds to an energy of position equal to 14·7. The kilogramme has, therefore, at this moment a total energy of 19·6, of which 14·7 units are due to position, and 4·9 to actual motion.

If we next examine it at the end of another second, we shall find that it has just been brought to rest, so that its energy of motion is *nil*; nevertheless, it has succeeded in raising itself 19·6 metres in height, so that its energy of position is 19·6.

There is, therefore, no disappearance of energy during the rise of the kilogramme, but merely a gradual change from one kind to another. It starts with actual energy, and this is gradually changed into that of position; but if, at any stage of its ascent, we add together the actual energy of the kilogramme, and that due to its position, we shall find that their sum always remains the same.

39. Precisely the reverse takes place when the kilogramme begins its descent. It starts on its downward journey with no energy of motion whatever, but with a certain amount of energy of position; as it falls, its energy of position becomes less, and its actual energy greater, the sum of the two remaining constant throughout, until, when it is about to strike the ground, its energy of position has been entirely changed into that of actual motion, and it now approaches the ground with the velocity, and, therefore, with the energy, which it had when it was originally projected upwards.

The Inclined Plane.

40. We have thus traced the transmutations, as regards energy, of a kilogramme shot vertically upwards, and allowed to fall again to the earth, and we may now

MECHANICAL ENERGY AND ITS CHANGE INTO HEAT. 29

vary our hypothesis by making the kilogramme rise vertically, but descend by means of a smooth inclined plane without friction—imagine in fact, the kilogramme to be shaped like a ball or roller, and the plane to be perfectly smooth. Now, it is well known to all students of dynamics, that in such a case the velocity which the kilogramme has when it has reached the bottom of the plane will be equal to that which it would have had if it had been dropped down vertically through the same height, and thus, by introducing a smooth inclined plane of this kind, you neither gain nor lose anything as regards energy.

In the first place, you do not gain, for think what would happen if the kilogramme, when it reached the bottom of the inclined plane, should have a greater velocity than you gave it originally, when you shot it up. It would evidently be a profitable thing to shoot up the kilogramme vertically, and bring it down by means of the plane, for you would get back more energy than you originally spent upon it, and in every sense you would be a gainer. You might, in fact, by means of appropriate apparatus, convert the arrangement into a perpetual motion machine, and go on accumulating energy without limit—but this is not possible.

On the other hand, the inclined plane, unless it be rough and angular, will not rob you of any of the energy of the kilogramme, but will restore to you the full amount, when once the bottom has been reached. Nor does it matter what be the length or shape of the plane, or whether it be straight, or curved, or spiral, for in all cases, if it only be smooth and of the same vertical height, you will get the same amount of energy by causing the kilogramme to fall from the top to the bottom.

41. But while the energy remains the same, the time of descent will vary according to the length and shape of the plane, for evidently the kilogramme will take a longer time to descend a very sloping plane than a very steep one. In fact, the sloping plane will take longer to generate the requisite velocity than the steep one, but both will have produced the same result as regards energy, when once the kilogramme has arrived at the bottom.

Functions of a Machine.

42. Our readers are now beginning to perceive that energy cannot be created, and that by no means can we coax or cozen Dame Nature into giving us back more than we are entitled to get. To impress this fundamental principle still more strongly upon our minds, let us consider in detail one or two mechanical contrivances, and see what they amount to as regards energy.

Let us begin with the second system of pulleys. Here we have a power P attached to the one end of a thread, which passes

Fig. 1.

over all the pulleys, and is ultimately attached, by its other extremity, to a hook in the upper or fixed block. The weight W is, on the other hand, attached to the lower or moveable block, and rises with it. Let us suppose that the pulleys are without weight and the cords without friction, and that W is supported by six cords, as in the figure. Now, when there is equilibrium in this machine, it is well known that W will be equal to six times P; that is to say, a power of one kilogramme will, in such a machine, balance or support a weight of six kilogrammes. If P be increased a single grain more, it will overbalance W, and P will descend, while W will begin to rise. In such a case, after P has descended, say six metres, its weight being, say, one kilogramme, it has lost a quantity of energy of position equal to six units, since it is at a lower level by six metres than it was before. We have, in fact, expended upon our machine six units of energy. Now, what return have we received for this expenditure? Our return is clearly the rise of W, and mechanicians will tell us that in this case W will have risen one metre.

But the weight of W is six kilogrammes, and this having been raised one metre represents an energy of position equal to six. We have thus spent upon our machine, in the fall of P, an amount of energy equal to six units, and obtained in the rise of W an equivalent amount equal to six units also. We have, in truth, neither gained nor lost energy, but simply changed it into a form more convenient for our use.

43. To impress this truth still more strongly, let us take quite a different machine, such as the hydrostatic press. Its mode of action will be perceived from Fig. 2. Here we have two cylinders, a wide and a narrow one, which are connected together at the bottom by means of a strong tube. Each of these cylinders is provided with a water-tight piston, the space beneath being filled with water. It is therefore manifest, since the two cylinders are connected together, and since water is incompressible, that when we push down the one piston the other will be pushed up. Let us suppose that the area of the small piston is one square centimetre,* and that of the large piston one hundred square centimetres, and let us apply a weight of ten kilogrammes to the smaller piston. Now, it is known, from the laws of hydrostatics, that every square centimetre of the larger piston will be pressed upwards with the force of ten kilogrammes, so that the piston will altogether mount with the force of 1000 kilogrammes—that is to say, it will raise a weight of this amount as it ascends.

Fig. 2.

Here, then, we have a machine in virtue of which a pressure of ten kilogrammes on the small piston enables the large piston to rise with the force of 1000 kilo-

* That is to say, a square the side of which is one centimetre, or the hundredth part of a metre.

grammes. But it is very easy to see that, while the small piston falls one metre, the large one will only rise one centimetre. For the quantity of water under the pistons being always the same, if this be pushed down one metre in the narrow cylinder, it will only rise one centimetre in the wide one.

Let us now consider what we gain by this machine. The power of ten kilogrammes applied to the smaller piston is made to fall through one metre, and this represents the amount of energy which we have expended upon our machine, while, as a return, we obtain 1000 kilogrammes raised through one single centimetre. Here, then, as in the case of the pulleys, the return of energy is precisely the same as the expenditure, and, provided we ignore friction, we neither gain nor lose anything by the machine. All that we do is to transmute the energy into a more convenient form—what we gain in power we lose in space; but we are willing to sacrifice space or quickness of motion in order to obtain the tremendous pressure or force which we get by means of the hydrostatic press.

Principle of Virtual Velocities.

44. These illustrations will have prepared our readers to perceive the true function of a machine. This was first clearly defined by Galileo, who saw that in any machine, no matter of what kind, if we raise a large weight by means of a small one, it will be found that the small weight, multiplied into the space through which it

is lowered, will exactly equal the large weight, multiplied into that through which it is raised.

This principle, known as that of virtual velocities, enables us to perceive at once our true position. We see that the world of mechanism is not a manufactory, in which energy is created, but rather a mart, into which we may bring energy of one kind and change or barter it for an equivalent of another kind, that suits us better—but if we come with nothing in our hand, with nothing we shall most assuredly return. A machine, in truth, does not create, but only transmutes, and this principle will enable us to tell, without further knowledge of mechanics, what are the conditions of equilibrium of any arrangement.

For instance, let it be required to find those of a lever, of which the one arm is three times as long as the other. Here it is evident that if we overbalance the lever by a single grain, so as to cause the long arm with its power to fall down while the short one with its weight rises up, then the long arm will fall three inches for every inch through which the short arm rises; and hence, to make up for this, a single kilogramme on the long arm will balance three kilogrammes on the short one, or the power will be to the weight as one is to three.

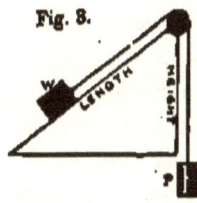

Fig. 3.

45. Or, again, let us take the inclined plane as represented in Fig. 3.

Here we have a smooth plane and a weight held upon it by means of a power P, as in the figure. Now, if we overbalance P by a single grain, we shall bring the weight W from the bottom to the top of the plane. But when this has taken place, it is evident that P has fallen through a vertical distance equal to the length of the plane, while on the other hand W has only risen through a vertical distance equal to the height. Hence, in order that the principle of virtual velocities shall hold, we must have P multiplied into its fall equal to W multiplied into its rise, that is to say,

$$P \times \text{Length of plane} = W \times \text{Height of plane,}$$
$$\text{or } \frac{P}{W} = \frac{\text{Height}}{\text{Length}}.$$

What Friction does.

46. The two examples now given are quite sufficient to enable our readers to see the true function of a machine, and they are now doubtless disposed to acknowledge that no machine will give back more energy than is spent upon it. It is not, however, equally clear that it will not give back less; indeed, it is a well-known fact that it constantly does so. For we have supposed our machine to be without friction—but no machine is without friction—and the consequence is that the available out-come of the machine is more or less diminished by this drawback. Now, unless we are able to see clearly

what part friction really plays, we cannot prove the conservation of energy. We see clearly enough that energy cannot be created, but we are not equally sure that it cannot be destroyed; indeed, we may say we have apparent grounds for believing that it is destroyed—that is our present position. Now, if the theory of the conservation of energy be true—that is to say, if energy is in any sense indestructible—friction will prove itself to be, not the destroyer of energy, but merely the converter of it into some less apparent and perhaps less useful form.

47. We must, therefore, prepare ourselves to study what friction really does, and also to recognize energy in a form remote from that possessed by a body in visible motion, or by a head of water. To friction we may add percussion, as a process by which energy is apparently destroyed; and as we have (Art. 39) considered the case of a kilogramme shot vertically upwards, demonstrating that it will ultimately reach the ground with an energy equal to that with which it was shot upwards, we may pursue the experiment one step further, and ask what becomes of its energy after it has struck the ground and come to rest? We may vary the question by asking what becomes of the energy of the smith's blow after his hammer has struck the anvil, or what of the energy of the cannon ball after it has struck the target, or what of that of the railway train after it has been stopped by friction at the break-wheel? All these

are cases in which percussion or friction appears at first sight to have destroyed visible energy; but before pronouncing upon this seeming destruction, it clearly behoves us to ask if anything else makes its appearance at the moment when the visible energy is apparently destroyed. For, after all, energy may be like the Eastern magicians, of whom we read that they had the power of changing themselves into a variety of forms, but were nevertheless very careful not to disappear altogether.

When Motion is destroyed, Heat appears.

48. Now, in reply to the question we have put, it may be confidently asserted that whenever visible energy is apparently destroyed by percussion or friction, something else makes its appearance, and that something is *heat*. Thus, a piece of lead placed upon an anvil may be greatly heated by successive blows of a blacksmith's hammer. The collision of flint and steel will produce heat, and a rapidly-moving cannon ball, when striking against an iron target, may even be heated to redness. Again, with regard to friction, we know that on a dark night sparks are seen to issue from the break-wheel which is stopping a railway train, and we know, also, that the axles of railway carriages get alarmingly hot, if they are not well supplied with grease.

Finally, the schoolboy will tell us that he is in the habit of rubbing a brass button upon the desk, and applying it to the back of his neighbour's hand, and that when his own hand has been treated in this way, he has found the button unmistakeably hot.

Heat a species of Motion.

49. For a long time this appearance of heat by friction or percussion was regarded as inexplicable, because it was believed that heat was a kind of matter, and it was difficult to understand where all this heat came from. The partisans of the material hypothesis, no doubt, ventured to suggest that in such processes heat might be drawn from the neighbouring bodies, so that the Caloric (which was the name given to the imaginary substance of heat) was squeezed or rubbed out of them, according as the process was percussion or friction. But this was regarded by many as no explanation, even before Sir Humphry Davy, about the end of last century, clearly showed it to be untenable.

50. Davy's experiments consisted in rubbing together two pieces of ice until it was found that both were nearly melted, and he varied the conditions of his experiments in such a manner as to show that the heat produced in this case could not be abstracted from the neighbouring bodies.

51. Let us pause to consider the alternatives to which we are driven by this experiment. If we still choose to regard heat as a substance, since this has not been taken from the surrounding bodies, it must necessarily have been created in the process of friction. But if we choose

to regard heat as a species of motion, we have a simpler alternative, for, inasmuch as the energy of visible motion has disappeared in the process of friction, we may suppose that it has been transformed into a species of molecular motion, which we call heat; and this was the conclusion to which Davy came.

52. About the same time another philosopher was occupied with a similar experiment. Count Rumford was superintending the boring of cannon at the arsenal at Munich, and was forcibly struck with the very great amount of heat caused by this process. The source of this heat appeared to him to be absolutely inexhaustible, and, being unwilling to regard it as the creation of a species of matter, he was led like Davy to attribute it to motion.

53. Assuming, therefore, that heat is a species of motion, the next point is to endeavour to comprehend what kind of motion it is, and in what respects it is different from ordinary visible motion. To do this, let us imagine a railway carriage, full of passengers, to be whirling along at a great speed, its occupants quietly at ease, because, although they are in rapid motion, they are all moving at the same rate and in the same direction. Now, suppose that the train meets with a sudden check;—a disaster is the consequence, and the quiet placidity of the occupants of the carriage is instantly at an end.

Even if we suppose that the carriage is not broken up and its occupants killed, yet they are all in a violent state of excitement; those fronting the engine are driven with force against their opposite neighbours, and are, no doubt, as forcibly repelled, each one taking care of himself in the general scramble. Now, we have only to substitute particles for persons, in order to obtain an idea of what takes place when percussion is converted into heat. We have, or suppose we have, in this act the same violent collision of atoms, the same thrusting forward of A upon B, and the same violence in pushing back on the part of B—the same struggle, confusion, and excitement—the only difference being that particles are heated instead of human beings, or their tempers.

54. We are bound to acknowledge that the proof which we have now given is not a direct one; indeed, we have, in our first chapter, explained the impossibility of our ever seeing these individual particles, or watching their movements; and hence our proof of the assertion that heat consists in such movements cannot possibly be direct. We cannot see that it does so consist, but yet we may feel sure, as reasonable beings, that we are right in our conjecture.

In the argument now given, we have only two alternatives to start with—either heat must consist of a motion of particles, or, when percussion or friction is converted into heat, a peculiar substance called caloric must be created, for if heat be not a species of motion it must necessarily be a species of matter. Now, we have preferred to consider heat as a species of motion to the alternative of supposing the creation of a peculiar kind of matter.

55. Nevertheless, it is desirable to have something to say to an opponent who, rather than acknowledge heat to be a species of motion, will allow the creation of matter. To such an one we would say that innumerable experiments render it certain that a hot body is not sensibly heavier than a cold one, so that if heat be a species of matter it is one that is not subject to the law of gravity. If we burn iron wire in oxygen gas, we are entitled to say that the iron combines with the oxygen, because we know that the product is heavier than the original iron by the very amount which the gas has lost in weight. But there is no such proof that during combustion the iron has combined with a substance called caloric, and the absence of any such proof is enough to entitle us to consider heat to be a species of motion, rather than a species of matter.

Heat a Backward and Forward Motion.

56. We shall now suppose that our readers have assented to our proposition that heat is a species of motion. It is almost unnecessary to add that it must be a species of backward and forward motion; for nothing is more clear than that *a heated substance is not in motion as a whole*, and will not, if put upon a table, push its way from the one end to the other.

Mathematicians express this peculiarity by saying that,

although there is violent internal motion among the particles, yet the centre of gravity of the substance remains at rest; and since, for most purposes, we may suppose a body to act as if concentrated at its centre of gravity, we may say that the body is at rest.

57. Let us here, before proceeding further, borrow an illustration from that branch of physics which treats of sound. Suppose, for instance, that a man is accurately balanced in a scale-pan, and that some water enters his ear; of course he will become heavier in consequence, and if the balance be sufficiently delicate, it will exhibit the difference. But suppose a sound or a noise enters his ear, he may say with truth that something has entered, but yet that something is not matter, nor will he become one whit heavier in consequence of its entrance, and he will remain balanced as before. Now, a man into whose ear sound has entered may be compared to a substance into which heat has entered; we may therefore suppose a heated body to be similar in many respects to a sounding body, and just as the particles of a sounding body move backwards and forwards, so we may suppose that the particles of a heated body do the same.

We shall take another opportunity (Art. 162) to enlarge upon this likeness; but, meanwhile, we shall suppose that our readers perceive the analogy.

Mechanical Equivalent of Heat.

58. We have thus come to the conclusion that when any heavy body, say a kilogramme weight, strikes the ground, the visible energy of the kilogramme is changed into heat; and now, having established the fact of a relationship between these two forms of energy, our next point is to ascertain according to what law the heating effect depends upon the height of fall. Let us, for instance, suppose that a kilogramme of water is allowed to drop from the height of 848 metres, and that we have the means of confining to its own particles and retaining there the heating effect produced. Now, we may suppose that its descent is accomplished in two stages; that, first of all, it falls upon a platform from the height of 424 metres, and gets heated in consequence, and that then the heated mass is allowed to fall other 424 metres. It is clear that the water will now be doubly heated; or, in other words, the heating effect in such a case will be proportional to the height through which the body falls—that is to say, it will be proportional to the actual energy which the body possesses before the blow has changed this into heat. In fact, just as the actual energy represented by a fall from a height is proportional to the height, so is the heating effect, or molecular energy, into which the actual energy is changed proportional to the height also. Having established this point, we now wish to know through

how many metres a kilogramme of water must fall in order to be heated one degree centigrade.

59. For a precise determination of this important point, we are indebted to Dr. Joule, of Manchester, who has, perhaps, done more than any one else to put the science of energy upon a sure foundation. Dr. Joule made numerous experiments, with the view of arriving at the exact relation between mechanical energy and heat; that is to say, of determining the mechanical equivalent of heat. In some of the most important of these he took advantage of the friction of fluids.

60. These experiments were conducted in the following manner. A certain fixed weight was attached to a pulley, as in the figure. The weight had, of course, a tendency

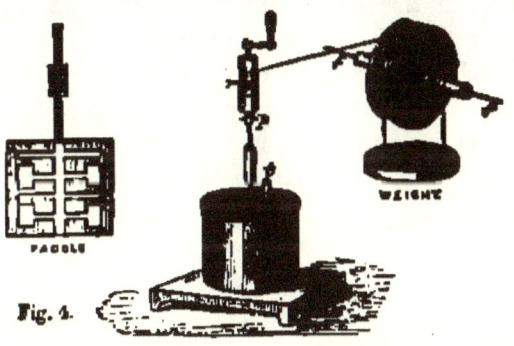

Fig. 4.

to descend, and hence to turn the pulley round. The pulley had its axle supported upon friction wheels, at f and f, by means of which the friction caused by the movement of the pulley was very much reduced. A string, passing over the circumference of the pulley, was wrapped round r, so that, as the weight descended, the pulley moved round, and the string of the pulley caused r to rotate very rapidly. Now, the motion of the axis r was conducted within the covered box B, where there was attached to r a system of paddles, of which a sketch is given in figure; and therefore, as r moved, these paddles moved also. There were, altogether, eight sets of these paddles revolving between four stationary vanes. If, therefore, the box were full of liquid, the paddles and the vanes together would churn it about, for these stationary vanes would prevent the liquid being carried along by the paddles in the direction of rotation.

Now, in this experiment, the weight was made to descend through a certain fixed distance, which was accurately measured. As it descended, the paddles were set in motion, and the energy of the descending weight was thus made to churn, and hence to heat some water contained in the box B. When the weight had descended a certain distance, by undoing a small peg p, it could be wound up again without moving the paddles in B, and thus the heating effect of several falls of the weight could be accumulated until this became so great as to be capable of being accurately measured by a thermometer. It ought to be mentioned that great care was taken in these experiments, not only to reduce the friction of the axles of the pulley as much as possible, but also to estimate and correct for this friction as accurately as possible; in fact, every precaution was taken to make the experiment successful.

61. Other experiments were made by Joule, in some of which a disc was made to rotate against another disc of cast-iron pressed against it, the whole arrangement being immersed in a cast-iron vessel filled with mercury. From all these experiments, Dr. Joule concluded that the quantity of heat produced by friction, if we can preserve and accurately measure it, will always be found proportional to the quantity of work expended. He expressed this proportion by stating the number of units of work in kilogrammetres necessary to raise by 1° C. the temperature of one kilogramme of water. This was 424, as determined by his last and most complete experiments; and hence we may conclude that if a kilogramme of water be allowed to fall through 424 metres, and if its motion be then suddenly stopped, sufficient heat will be generated to raise the temperature of the water through 1° C., and so on, in the same proportion.

62. Now, if we take the kilogrammetre as our unit of work, and the heat necessary to raise a kilogramme of water 1° C. as our unit of heat, this proportion may be expressed by saying that *one heat unit is equal to 424 units of work.*

This number is frequently spoken of as the mechanical equivalent of heat; and in scientific treatises it is denoted by J., the initial of Dr. Joule's name.

63. We have now stated the exact relationship that subsists between mechanical energy and heat, and before proceeding further with proofs of the great law of conservation, we shall endeavour to make our readers acquainted with other varieties of energy, on the ground that it is necessary to penetrate the various disguises that our magician assumes before we can pretend to explain the principles that actuate him in his transformations.

CHAPTER III.

THE FORCES AND ENERGIES OF NATURE: THE LAW OF CONSERVATION.

64. In the last chapter we introduced our readers to two varieties of energy, one of them visible, and the other invisible or molecular; and it will now be our duty to search through the whole field of physical science for other varieties. Here it is well to bear in mind that all energy consists of two kinds, that of *position* and that of *actual motion*, and also that this distinction holds for invisible molecular energy just as truly as it does for that which is visible. Now, energy of position implies a body in a position of advantage with respect to some force, and hence we may with propriety begin our search by investigating the various forces of nature.

Gravitation.

65. The most general, and perhaps the most important, of these forces is *gravitation*, and the law of action of this force may be enunciated as follows:—*Every particle of the universe attracts every other particle with a force*

depending jointly upon the mass of the attracting and of the attracted particle, and varying inversely as the square of distance between the two. A little explanation will make this plain.

Suppose a particle or system of particles of which the mass is unity to be placed at a distance equal to unity from another particle or system of particles of which the mass is also unity—the two will attract each other. Let us agree to consider the mutual attraction between them equal to unity also.

Suppose, now, that we have on the one side two such systems with a mass represented by 2, and on the other side the same system as before, with a mass represented by unity, the distance, meanwhile, remaining unaltered. It is clear the double system will now attract the single system with a twofold force. Let us next suppose the mass of both systems to be doubled, the distance always remaining the same. It is clear that we shall now have a fourfold force, each unit of the one system attracting each unit of the other. In like manner, if the mass of the one system is 2, and that of the other 3, the force will be 6. We may, for instance, call the components of the one system A_1, A_2, and those of the other A_3, A_4, A_5, and we shall have A_1 pulled towards $A_3, A_4,$ and A_5 with a threefold force, and A_2 pulled towards $A_3, A_4,$ and A_5 with a threefold force, making altogether a force equal to 6.

In the next place, let the masses remain unaltered, but let the distance between them be doubled, then the force will be reduced fourfold. Let the distance be tripled, then the force will be reduced ninefold, and so on.

66. Gravitation may be described as a very weak force, capable of acting at a distance, or at least of appearing to do so. It takes the mass of the whole earth to produce the force with which we are so familiar at its surface, and the presence of a large mass of rock or mountain does not produce any appreciable difference in the weight of any substance. It is the gravitation of the earth, lessened of course by distance, which acts upon the moon 240,000 miles away, and the gravitation of the sun influences in like manner the earth and the various other planets of our system.

Elastic Forces.

67. Elastic forces, although in their mode of action very different from gravity, are yet due to visible arrangements of matter; thus, when a cross-bow is bent, there is a visible change produced in the bow, which, as a whole, resists this bending, and tends to resume its previous position. It therefore requires energy to bend a bow, just as truly and visibly as it does to raise a weight above the earth, and elasticity is, therefore, as truly a species of force as gravity is. We shall not here attempt to discuss the various ways in which this force may act, or in which a solid elastic substance will resist

all attempts to deform it; but in all cases it is clearly manifest that work must be spent upon the body, and the force of elasticity must be encountered and overcome throughout a certain space before any sensible deformation can take place.

Force of Cohesion.

68. Let us now leave the forces which animate large masses of matter, and proceed to discuss those which subsist between the smaller particles of which these large masses are composed. And here we must say one word more about molecules and atoms, and the distinction we feel ourselves entitled to draw between these very small bodies, even although we shall never be able to see either the one or the other.

In our first chapter (Art. 7) we supposed the continual sub-division of a grain of sand until we had arrived at the smallest entity retaining all the properties of sand —this we called a *molecule*, and nothing smaller than this is entitled to be called sand. If we continue this sub-division further, the molecule of sand separates itself into its chemical constituents, consisting of silicon on the one side, and oxygen on the other. Thus we arrive at last at the smallest body which can call itself silicon, and the smallest which can call itself oxygen, and we have no reason to suppose that either of these is capable of sub-division into something else, since we regard oxygen and silicon as elementary or simple bodies. Now, these constituents of the silicon molecule are called *atoms*, so that we say the sand molecule is divisible into atoms of silicon and of oxygen. Furthermore, we have strong reason for supposing that such molecules and atoms really exist, but into the arguments for their existence we cannot now enter—it is one of those things that we must ask our readers to take for granted.

69. Let us now take two molecules of sand. These, when near together, have a very strong attraction for each other. It is, in truth, this attraction which renders it difficult to break up a crystalline particle of sand or rock crystal. But it is only exerted when the molecules are near enough together to form a homogeneous crystalline structure, for let the distance between them be somewhat increased, and we find that all attraction entirely vanishes. Thus there is little or no attraction between different particles of sand, even although they are very closely packed together. In like manner, the integrity of a piece of glass is due to the attraction between its molecules; but let these be separated by a flaw, and it will soon be found that this very small increase of distance greatly diminishes the attraction between the particles, and that the structure will now fall to pieces from the slightest cause. Now, these examples are sufficient to show that molecular attraction or *cohesion*, as this is called, is a force which acts very powerfully through a certain small distance, but which vanishes altogether when this distance becomes perceptible. Cohesion is

strongest in solids, while in liquids it is much diminished, and in gases it may be said to vanish altogether. The molecules of gases are, in truth, so far away from one another, as to have little or no mutual attraction, a fact proved by Dr. Joule, whose name was mentioned in the last chapter.

Force of Chemical Affinity.

70. Let us now consider the mutual forces between atoms. These may be characterized as even stronger than the forces between molecules, but as disappearing still more rapidly when the distance is increased. Let us, for instance, take carbon and oxygen—two substances which are ready to combine together to form carbonic acid, whenever they have a suitable opportunity. In this case, each atom of carbon will unite with two of oxygen, and the result will be something quite different from either. Yet under ordinary circumstances carbon, or its representative, coal, will remain unchanged in the presence of oxygen, or of atmospheric air containing oxygen. There will be no tendency to combine together, because although the particles of the oxygen would appear to be in immediate contact with those of the carbon, yet the nearness is not sufficient to permit of chemical affinity acting with advantage. When, however, the nearness becomes sufficient, then chemical affinity begins to operate. We have, in fact, the familiar act of combustion, and, as its consequence, the chemical union of the

carbon or coal with the oxygen of the air, carbonic acid being the result. Here, then, we have a very powerful force acting only at a very small distance, which we name *chemical affinity*, inasmuch as it represents the attraction exerted between atoms of different bodies in contradistinction to cohesion, which denotes the attraction between molecules of the same body.

71. If we regard gravitation as the representative of forces that act or appear to act, at a distance, we may regard cohesion and chemical affinity as the representatives of those forces which, although very powerful, only act or appear to act through a very small interval of distance.

A little reflection will show us how inconvenient it would be if gravitation diminished very rapidly with the distance; for then even supposing that the bond which retains us to the earth were to hold good, that which retains the moon to the earth might vanish entirely, as well as that which retains the earth to the sun, and the consequences would be far from pleasant. Reflection will also show us how inconvenient it would be if chemical affinity existed at all distances; if coal, for instance, were to combine with oxygen without the application of heat, it would greatly alter the value of this fuel to mankind, and would materially check the progress of human industry.

THE FORCES AND ENERGIES OF NATURE. 55

Remarks on Molecular and Atomic Forces.

72. Now, it is important to remember that we must treat cohesion and chemical affinity exactly in the same way as gravity has been treated; and just as we have energy of position with respect to gravity, so may we have as truly a species of energy of position with respect to cohesion and chemical affinity. Let us begin with cohesion.

73. We have hitherto regarded heat as a peculiar motion of the molecules of matter, without any reference to the force which actuates these molecules. But it is a well-known fact that bodies in general expand when heated, so that, in virtue of this expansion, the molecules of a body are driven violently apart against the force of cohesion. Work has in truth been done against this force, just as truly as, when a kilogramme is raised from the earth, work is done against the force of gravity. When a substance is heated, we may, therefore, suppose that the heat has a twofold office to perform, part of it going to increase the actual motions of the molecules, and part of it to separate these molecules from one another against the force of cohesion. Thus, if I swing round horizontally a weight (attached to my hand by an elastic thread of india-rubber), my energy will be spent in two ways—first of all, it will be spent in communicating a velocity to the weight; and, secondly, in stretching the india-rubber string, by means of the

centrifugal tendency of the weight. Work will be done against the elastic force of the string, as well as spent in increasing the motion of the weight.

Now, something of this kind may be taking place when a body is heated, for we may very well suppose heat to consist of a vertical or circular motion, the tendency of which would be to drive the particles asunder against the force of cohesion. Part, therefore, of the energy of heat will be spent in augmenting the motion, and part in driving asunder the particles. We may, however, suppose that, in ordinary cases, the great proportion of the energy of heat goes towards increasing the molecular motion, rather than in doing work against the force of cohesion.

74. In certain cases, however, it is probable that the greater part of the heat applied is spent in doing work against molecular forces, instead of increasing the motions of molecules.

Thus, when a solid melts, or when a liquid is rendered gaseous, a considerable amount of heat is spent in the process, which does not become sensible, that is to say, does not affect the thermometer. Thus, in order to melt a kilogramme of ice, heat is required sufficient to raise a kilogramme of water through 80° C., and yet, when melted, the water is no warmer than the ice. We express this fact by saying that the latent heat of water is 80. Again, if a kilogramme of water at 100° be converted entirely into steam, as much heat is required as would raise the water through 537° C., or 537 kilogrammes of water through one degree; but yet the steam is no hotter than the water, and we express this fact by saying that the latent heat of steam is 537. Now, in both of these instances it is at least extremely probable that a large portion of the heat is spent in doing work against the force of cohesion; and, more especially, when a fluid is converted into a gas, we know that the molecules are in that process separated so far from one another as to lose entirely any trace of mutual force. We may, therefore, conclude that although in most cases the greater portion of the heat applied to a body is spent in increasing its molecular motion, and only a small part in doing work against cohesion, yet when a solid melts, or a liquid vaporizes, a large portion of the heat required is not improbably spent in doing work against molecular forces. But the energy, though spent, is not lost, for when the liquid again freezes, or when the vapour again condenses, this energy is once more transformed into the shape of sensible heat, just as when a stone is dropped from the top of a house, its energy of position is transformed once more into actual energy.

75. A single instance will suffice to give our readers a notion of the strength of molecular forces. If a bar of wrought iron, whose temperature is 10° C. above that of the surrounding medium, be tightly secured at its extremities, it will draw these together with a force of at least one ton for each square inch of section. In some

cases where a building has shown signs of bulging outwards, iron bars have been placed across it, and secured while in a heated state to the walls. On cooling, the iron contracted with great force, and the walls were thereby pulled together.

76. We are next brought to consider atomic forces, or those which lead to chemical union, and now let us see how these are influenced by heat. We have seen that heat causes a separation between the molecules of a body, that is to say, it increases the distance between two contiguous molecules, but we must not suppose that, meanwhile, the molecules themselves are left unaltered.

The tendency of heat to cause separation is not confined to increasing the distance between molecules, but acts also, no doubt, in increasing the distance between parts of the same molecule: in fact, the energy of heat is spent in pulling the constituent atoms asunder against the force of chemical affinity, as well as in pulling the molecules asunder against the force of cohesion, so that, at a very high temperature, it is probable that most chemical compounds would be decomposed, and many are so, even at a very moderate heat.

Thus the attraction between oxygen and silver is so slight that at a comparatively low temperature the oxide of silver is decomposed. In like manner, limestone, or carbonate of lime, is decomposed when subjected to the heat of a lime-kiln, carbonic acid being given off, while quick-lime remains behind. Now, in separating heterogeneous atoms against the powerful force of chemical affinity, work is done as truly as it is in separating molecules from one another against the force of cohesion, or in separating a stone from the earth against the force of gravity.

77. Heat, as we have seen, is very frequently influential in performing this separation, and its energy is spent in so doing; but other energetic agents produce chemical decomposition as well as heat. For instance, certain rays of the sun decompose carbonic acid into carbon and oxygen in the leaves of plants, and their energy is spent in the process; that is to say, it is spent in pulling asunder two such powerfully attracting substances against the affinity they have for one another. And, again, the electric current is able to decompose certain substances, and of course its energy is spent in the process.

Therefore, whenever two powerfully attracting atoms are separated, energy is spent in causing this separation as truly as in separating a stone from the earth, and when once the separation has been accomplished we have a species of energy of position just as truly as we have in a head of water, or in a stone at the top of a house.

78. It is this chemical separation that is meant when we speak of coal as a source of energy. Coal, or carbon, has a great attraction for oxygen, and whenever heat is applied the two bodies unite together. Now oxygen, as it exists in the atmosphere, is the common inheritance of all, and if, in addition to this, some of us possess coal in our cellars, or in pits, we have thus secured a store of

energy of position which we can draw upon with more facility than if it were a head of water, for, although we can draw upon the energy of a head of water whenever we choose, yet we cannot carry it about with us from place to place as we can with coal. We thus perceive that it is not the coal, by itself, that forms the source of energy, but this is due to the fact that we have coal, or carbon, in one place, and oxygen in another, while we have also the means of causing them to unite with each other whenever we wish. If there were no oxygen in the air, coal by itself would be of no value.

Electricity: its Properties.

79. Our readers have now been told about the force of cohesion that exists between molecules of the same body, and also about that of chemical affinity existing between atoms of different bodies. Now, heterogeneity is an essential element of this latter force—there must be a difference of some kind before it can exhibit itself—and under these circumstances its exhibitions are frequently characterized by very extraordinary and interesting phenomena.

We allude to that peculiar exhibition arising out of the forces of heterogenous bodies which we call *electricity*, and, before proceeding further, it may not be out of place to give a short sketch of the mode of action of this very mysterious, but most interesting, agent.

80. The science of electricity is of very ancient origin;

but its beginning was very small. For a couple of thousand years it made little or no progress, and then, during the course of little more than a century, developed into the giant which it now is. The ancient Greeks were aware that amber, when rubbed with silk, had the property of attracting light bodies; and Dr. Gilbert, about three hundred years ago, showed that many other things, such as sulphur, sealing-wax, and glass, have the same property as amber.

In the progress of the science it came to be known that certain substances are able to carry away the peculiar influence produced, while others are unable to do so; the former are called *conductors*, and the latter *non-conductors, or insulators*, of electricity. To make the distinction apparent, let us take a metal rod, having a glass stem attached to it, and rub the glass stem with a piece of silk, care being taken that both silk and glass are warm and dry. We shall find that the glass has now acquired the property of attracting little bits of paper, or elder pith; but only where it has been rubbed, for the peculiar influence acquired by the glass has not been able to spread itself over the surface.

If, however, we take hold of the glass stem, and rub the metal rod, we may, perhaps, produce the same property in the metal, but it will spread over the whole, not confining itself to the part rubbed. Thus we perceive that metal is a conductor, while glass is an insulator, or non-conductor, of electricity.

81. We would next observe that *this influence is of two kinds*. To prove this, let us perform the following experiment. Let us suspend a small pith ball by a very slender silk thread, as in Fig. 5. Next, let us rub a stick of warm, dry glass with a piece of warm silk, and with this excited stick touch the pith ball. The pith ball, after being touched, will be repelled by the excited glass. Let us next excite, in a similar manner, a stick of dry sealing-wax with a piece of warm, dry flannel, and on approaching this stick to the pith ball it will attract it, although the ball, in its present state, is repelled by the excited glass.

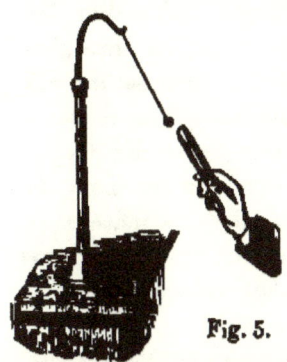

Fig. 5.

Thus a pith ball, touched by excited glass, is repelled by excited glass, but attracted by excited sealing-wax.

In like manner, it might be shown that a pith ball, touched by excited sealing-wax, will be afterwards repelled by excited sealing-wax, but attracted by excited glass.

Now, what the excited glass did to the pith ball was to communicate to it part of its own influence, after which the ball was repelled by the glass; or, in other words, *bodies charged with similar electricities repel one another*.

Again, since the pith ball, when charged with the electricity from glass, was attracted to the electrified sealing-wax, we conclude that *bodies charged with unlike electricities attract one another.* The electricity from glass is sometimes called *vitreous*, and that from sealing-wax *resinous*, electricity, but more frequently the former is known as *positive*, and the latter as *negative*, electricity—it being understood that these words do not imply the possession of a positive nature by the one influence, or of a negative nature by the other, but are merely terms employed to express the apparent antagonism which exists between the two kinds of electricity.

82. The next point worthy of notice is that *whenever one electricity is produced, just as much is produced of an opposite description.* Thus, in the case of glass excited by silk, we have positive electricity developed upon the glass, while we have also negative electricity developed upon the silk to precisely the same extent. And, again, when sealing-wax is rubbed with flannel, we have negative electricity developed upon the sealing-wax, and just as much positive upon the flannel.

83. These facts have given rise to a theory of electricity, or at least to a method of regarding it, which, if not absolutely correct, seems yet to unite together the various phenomena. According to this hypothesis, a neutral, unexcited body is supposed to contain a store of the two electricities combined together, so that whenever such a body is excited, a separation is produced

between the two. The phenomena which we have described are, therefore, due to this electrical separation, and inasmuch as the two electricities have a great affinity for one another, it requires the expenditure of energy to produce this separation, just as truly as it does to separate a stone from the earth.

84. Now, it is worthy of note that *electrical separation is only produced when heterogeneous bodies are rubbed together.* Thus, if flannel be rubbed upon glass, we have electricity; but if flannel be rubbed upon glass covered with flannel, we have none. In like manner, if silk be rubbed upon sealing-wax covered with silk, or, in fine, if two portions of the same substance be rubbed together, we have no electricity.

On the other hand, a very slight difference of texture is sometimes sufficient to produce electrical separation. Thus, if two pieces of the same silk ribbon be rubbed together lengthwise, we have no electricity; but if they be rubbed across each other, the one is positively, and the other negatively, electrified.

In fact, this element of heterogeneity is an all important one in electrical development, and this leads us to conjecture that *electrical attraction may probably be regarded as peculiarly allied to that force which we call chemical affinity.* At any rate, electricity and chemical affinity are only manifested between bodies that are, in some respects, dissimilar.

85. The following is a list of bodies arranged according

to the electricity which they develop when rubbed together, each substance being positively electrified when rubbed with any substance beneath it in the list.

1. Cat's skin.
2. Flannel.
3. Ivory.
4. Glass.
5. Silk.
6. Wood.
7. Shellac.
8. Resin.
9. Metals.
10. Sulphur.
11. Caoutchouc.
12. Gutta-percha.
13. Gun-cotton.

Thus, if resin be rubbed with cat's skin, or with flannel, the cat's skin or flannel will be positively, and the resin negatively, electrified; while if glass be rubbed with silk, the glass will be positively, and the silk negatively, electrified, and so on.

86. It is not our purpose here to describe at length the *electrical machine*, but we may state that it consists of two parts, one for generating electricity by means of the friction of a rubber against glass, and another consisting of a system of brass tubes, of considerable surface, supported on glass stems, for collecting and retaining the electricity so produced. This latter part of the machine is called its *prime conductor*.

Electric Induction.

87. Let us now suppose that we have set in action a machine of this kind, and accumulated a considerable

quantity of positive electricity in its prime conductor at A. Let us next take two vessels, B and C, made of brass

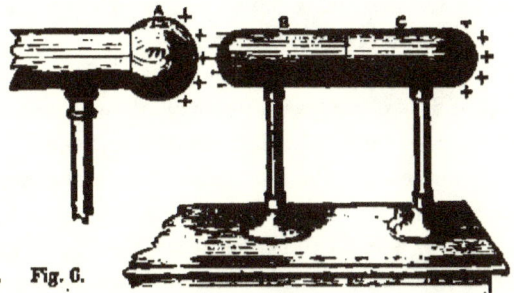

Fig. 6.

supported on glass stems. These two vessels are supposed to be in contact, but at the same time to be capable of being separated from one another at their middle point, where the line is drawn in Fig. 6. Now let us cause B and C to approach A together. At first, B and C are not electrified, that is to say, their two electricities are not separated from each other, but are mixed together; but mark what will happen as they are pushed towards A. The positive electricity of A will decompose the two electricities of B and C, attracting the negative towards itself, and repelling the positive as far away as possible. The disposition of electricities will, therefore, be as in the figure. If we now pull C away from B, we have obtained a quantity of positive electricity on C, by help of the original electricity which was in A; in fact, we have made use of the original stock or electrical capital in A, in order to obtain positive electricity in C, without, however, diminishing the amount of our original stock. Now, this distant action or help, rendered by the original electricity in separating that of B and C, is called electric induction.

88. The experiment may, however, be performed in a somewhat different manner—we may allow B and C to remain together, and gradually push them nearer to A. As B and C approach A, the separation of their electricities will become greater and greater, until, when A and B are only divided by a small thickness of air, the two opposite electricities then accumulated will have sufficient strength to rush together through the air, and unite with each other by means of a spark.

89. The principle of induction may be used with advantage, when it is wished to accumulate a large quantity of electricity.

In this case, an instrument called a *Leyden jar* is very frequently employed. It consists of a glass jar, coated inside and outside with tin foil, as in Fig. 7. A brass rod, having a knob at the end of it, is connected metallically with the inside coating, and is kept in its place by being passed through a cork, which covers the mouth of the jar. We have thus two metallic coatings which are not electrically connected with one another. Now, in order to charge a jar of this kind, let the outside coating be con-

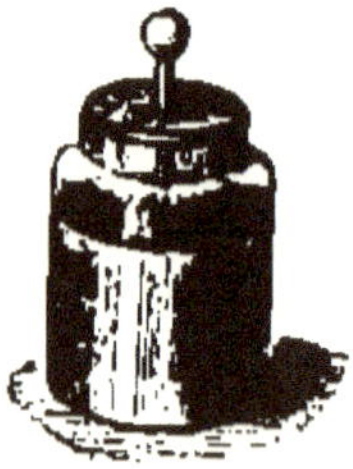

Fig. 7.

nected by a chain with the earth, while at the same time positive electricity from the prime conductor of an electrical machine is communicated to the inside knob.

The positive electricity will accumulate on the inside coating with which the knob is connected. It will then decompose the two electricities of the outside coating, driving the positive electricity to the earth, and there dissipating it, but attracting the negative to itself. There will thus be positive electricity on the inside, and negative on the outside coating. These two electricities may be compared to two hostile armies watching each other, and very anxious to get together, while, however, they are separated from one another by means of an insurmountable obstacle. They will thus remain facing each other, and at their posts, while each side is, meanwhile, being recruited by the same operation as before. We may by this means accumulate a vast quantity of opposite electricities on the two coatings of such a jar, and they will remain there for a long time, especially if the surrounding atmosphere and the glass surface of the jar be quite dry. When, however, electric connection of any kind is made between the two coatings, the electricities rush together and unite with one another in the shape of a spark, while if the human body be the instrument of connecting them a severe shock will be felt.

90. It would thus appear that, when two bodies charged with opposite electricities are brought near each other, the two electricities rush together, forming

a current, and the ultimate result is a spark. Now, this spark implies heat, and is, in truth, nothing else than small particles of intensely heated matter of some kind. We have here, therefore, first of all, the conversion of electrical separation into a current of electricity, and, secondly, the conversion of this current into heat. In this case, however, the current lasts only a very small time; the discharge, as it is called, of a Leyden jar being probably accomplished in $\frac{1}{1000}$th of a second.

The Electric Current.

91. In other cases we have electrical currents which, although not so powerful as that produced by discharging a Leyden jar, yet last longer, and are, in fact, continuous instead of momentary.

We may see a similar difference in the case of visible energy. Thus we might, by means of gunpowder, send up in a moment an enormous mass of water; or we might, by means of a fountain, send up the same mass in the course of time, and in a very much quieter manner. We have the same sort of difference in electrical discharges, and having spoken of the rushing together of two opposite electricities by means of an explosion and a spark, let us now speak of the eminently quiet and effective *voltaic current*, in which we have a continuous coming together of the same two agents.

92. It is not our object here to give a complete description, either historical or scientific, of the voltaic

battery, but rather to give such an account as will enable our readers to understand what the arrangement is, and what sort of effect it produces; and with this object we shall at once proceed to describe the battery of Grove, which is perhaps the most efficacious of all the various arrangements for the purpose of producing an electric current. In this battery we have a number of cells connected together, as in Fig. 8, which shows a battery of three cells. Each cell consists of two vessels, an outer and an inner one; the outer vessel being made of glass or ordinary stone ware, while the inner one is made of unglazed porcelain, and is therefore porous. The outer vessel is filled with dilute sulphuric acid, and a plate of amalgamated zinc—that is to say, of metallic zinc having its outer surface brightened with mercury,—is immersed in this acid. Again, in the inner or porous vessel we have strong nitric acid, in which a plate of platinum foil is immersed, this being at the same time electrically connected with the zinc plate of the next outer vessel, by means of a clamp, as in the figure. Both metals must be clean where they are pressed together, that is to say, the true metallic surfaces of both must be in contact. Finally, a wire is metallically connected with the platinum of the left-hand cell, and a similar wire with the

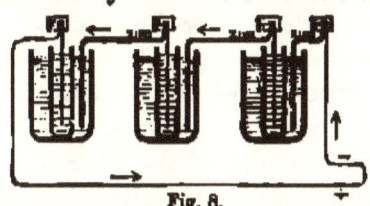

Fig. 8.

zinc of the right-hand cell, and these connecting wires ought, except at their extremities, to be covered over with gutta-percha or thread. The loose extremities of these wires are called the *poles* of the battery.

93. Let us now suppose that we have a battery containing a good many cells of this description, and let the whole arrangement be insulated, by being set upon glass supports, or otherwise separated from the earth. If now we test, by appropriate methods, the extremity of the wire connected with the left-hand platinum plate, it will be found to be charged with positive electricity, while the extremity of the other wire will be found charged with negative electricity.

94. In the next place, if we connect these poles of the battery with one another, the two electricities will rush together and unite, or, in other words, there will be an electric current; but it will not be a momentary but a continuous one, and for some time, provided these poles are kept together, a current of electricity will pass through the wires, and indeed through the whole arrangement, including the cells.

The direction of the current will be such that *positive electricity may be supposed to pass from the zinc to the platinum, through the liquid; and back again through the wire, from the platinum at the left hand, to the zinc at the right;* in fact, to go in the direction indicated by the arrow-head.

95. Thus we have two things. In the first place, before

the two terminals, or poles, have been brought together, we have them charged with opposite electricities; and, secondly, when once they have been brought together, we have the production of a continuous current of electricity. Now, this current is an energetic agent, in proof of which we shall proceed to consider the various properties which it has,—the various things which it can do.

Its Magnetic Effects.

96. In the first place, *it can deflect the magnetic needle.* For instance, let a compass needle be swung freely, and let a current of electricity circulate along a wire placed near this needle, and in the direction of its length, then the direction in which the needle points will be immediately altered. This direction will now depend upon that of the current, conveyed by the wire, and the needle will endeavour to place itself at right angles to this wire.

In order to remember the connection between the direction of the current and that of the magnet, imagine your body to form part of the positive current, which may be supposed to enter in at your head, and go out at your feet; also imagine that your face is turned towards the magnet. In this case, the pole of the magnet, which points to the north, will always be deflected by the current towards your right hand. The strength of a current may be measured by the amount of the deflection it produces upon a magnetic needle, and the instrument by which this measurement is made is called a *galvanometer*.

97. In the next place, *the current is able*, not merely to deflect a magnet, but also *to render soft iron magnetic*.

Let us take, for instance, the wire connected with the one pole of the battery, and cover it with thread, in order to insulate it and let us wrap this wire round a cylinder of soft iron, as in Fig. 9. If we now make a communication between the other extremity of the wire, and the other pole of the battery, so as to make the current pass, it will be found that our cylinder of soft iron has become a powerful magnet, and that if an iron keeper be attached to it as in the figure, the keeper will be able to sustain a very great weight.

Fig. 9.

Its Heating Effect.

98. *The electric current has likewise the property of heating a wire through which it passes.* To prove this, let us connect the two poles of a battery by means of a fine platinum wire, when it will be found that the wire will, in a few seconds, become heated to redness. In point of fact, the current will heat a thick wire, but not so much as a thin one, for we may suppose it to rush with great violence through the limited section of the thin wire, producing in its passage great heat.

Its Chemical Effect.

99. Besides its magnetic and heating effects, *the current has also the power of decomposing compound substances, under certain conditions.* Suppose, for instance, that the poles of a battery, instead of being brought together, are plunged into a vessel of water, decomposition will at once begin, and small bubbles of oxygen will rise from the positive pole, while small bubbles of hydrogen will make their appearance at the negative. If the two gases are collected together in a vessel, they may be exploded, and if collected separately, it may be proved by the ordinary tests, that the one is oxygen and the other hydrogen.

Attraction and Repulsion of Currents.

100. We have now described very shortly the magnetic, the heating, and the chemical effects of currents; it remains for us to describe the effects of currents upon one another.

In the first place, suppose that we have two wires which are parallel to one another, and carry currents going in the same direction; and let us further suppose that these wires are capable of moving, then it is found that they will attract one another. If, however, the wires, although parallel, convey currents going in opposite directions, they will then repel one another. A good way of showing this experimentally is to cause two circular currents to float on water. If these currents both go either in the same direction as the hands of a watch, or in the opposite direction, then the two will attract one another; but if the one goes in the one direction, and the other in the other, they will then repel one another.

Attraction and Repulsion of Magnets.

101. Ampère, who discovered this property of currents, has likewise shown us that in very many respects a magnet may be likened to a collection of circular currents all parallel to one another, their direction being such that, if you look towards the north pole of a freely suspended cylindrical magnet facing it, the positive current will descend on the east or left-hand side, and ascend on the west or right-hand side. If we adopt this method of viewing magnets, we can easily account for the attraction between the unlike and the repulsion between the like poles of a magnet, for when unlike poles are placed near each other, the circular currents which face each other are then all going in the same direction, and the two will, therefore, attract one another, but if like poles are placed in this position, the currents that face each other are going in opposite directions, and the poles will, therefore, repel one another.

Induction of Currents.

102. Before closing this short sketch of electrical phenomena, we must allude to the inductive effect of

currents upon each other. Let us suppose (Fig. 10) that

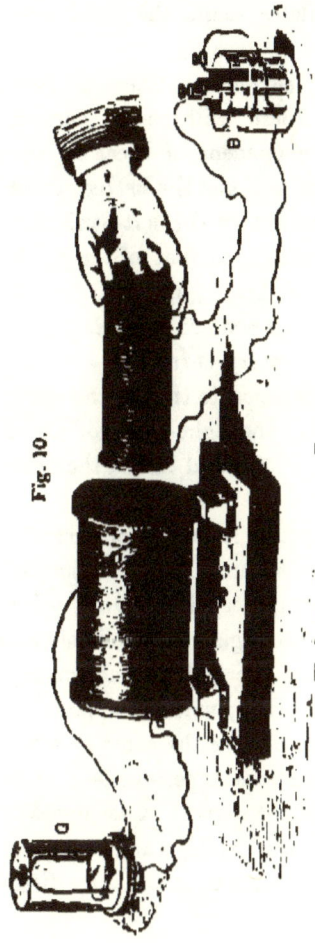

Fig. 10.

we have two circular coils of wire, covered with thread, and placed near each other. Let both the extremities of the right-hand coil be connected with the poles of a battery, so as to make a current of electricity circulate round the coil. On the other hand, let the left-hand coil be connected with a galvanometer, thus enabling us to detect the smallest current of electricity which may pass through this coil. Now, it is found that when we first connect the right-hand coil, so as to pass the battery current through it, a momentary current will pass through the left-hand coil, and will deflect the needle of the galvanometer, but this current will go in an opposite direction to that which circulates round the right-hand coil.

103. Again, as long as the current continues to flow through the right-hand coil there will be no current through the other, but at the moment of breaking the contact between the right-hand coil and the battery there will again be a momentary current in the left-hand coil, but this time in the same direction as that of the right-hand coil, instead of being, as before, in the opposite direction. In other words, when contact is *made* in the right-hand coil, there is a momentary current in the left-hand coil, but in an opposite direction to that in the right, while, when contact is *broken* in the right-hand coil, there is a momentary current in the left-hand coil in the same direction as that in the right.

104. In order to exemplify this induction of currents, it is not even necessary to make and break the current in the right-hand coil, for we may keep it constantly going and arrange so as to make the right-hand coil (always retaining its connection with the battery) alternately approach and recede from the other; when it approaches the other, the effect produced will be the same as when the contact was made in the above experiment—that is to say, we shall have an induced current in an opposite direction to that of the primary, while, when it recedes from the other, we shall have a current in the same direction as that of the primary.

105. Thus we see that whether we keep both coils stationary, and suddenly produce a current in the right-hand coil, or whether, keeping this current constantly going, we suddenly bring it near the other coil, the inductive effect will be precisely the same, for in both cases the left-hand coil is suddenly brought into the presence of a current. And again, it is the same, whether we suddenly break the right-hand current, or suddenly remove it from the left-hand coil, for in both cases this coil is virtually removed from the presence of a current.

List of Energies.

106. We are now in a position to enumerate the various kinds of energy which occur in nature; but, before doing so, we must warn our readers that this enumeration has nothing absolute or complete about it, representing, as it does, not so much the present state of our knowledge as of our want of knowledge, or rather profound ignorance, of the ultimate constitution of matter. It is, in truth, only a convenient classification, and nothing more.

107. To begin, then, with visible energy. We have first of all—

Energy of Visible Motion.

(A) Visible energy of actual motion—in the planets, in meteors, in the cannon ball, in the storm, in the running stream, and in other instances of bodies in actual visible motion, too numerous to be mentioned.

Visible Energy of Position.

(B.) We have also visible energy of position—in a stone on the top of a cliff, in a head of water, in a rain cloud, in a cross-bow bent, in a clock or watch wound up, and in various other instances.

108. Then we have, besides, several cases in which there is an alternation between (A) and (B).

A pendulum, for instance, when at its lowest point, has only the energy (A), or that of actual motion, in virtue of which it ascends a certain distance against the force of gravity. When, however, it has completed its ascent, its energy is then of the variety (B), being due to position, and not to actual motion; and so on it continues to oscillate, alternately changing the nature of its energy from (A) to (B), and from (B) back again to (A).

109. A vibrating body is another instance of this alternation. Each particle of such a body may be compared to an exceedingly small pendulum oscillating backwards and forwards, only very much quicker than an ordinary pendulum; and just as the ordinary pendulum in passing its point of rest has its energy all of one kind, while in passing its upper point it has it all of another, so when a vibrating particle is passing its point of rest, its energy is all of the variety (A), and when it has reached its extreme displacement, it is all of the variety (B).

Heat Motion.

110. (C.) Coming now to molecular or invisible energy, we have, in the first place, that motion of the molecules of bodies which we term heat. A better term would be *absorbed heat*, to distinguish it from *radiant heat*, which is a very different thing. That peculiar motion which is imparted by heat when absorbed into a body is, therefore, one variety of molecular energy.

Molecular Separation.

(D.) Analogous to this is that effect of heat which represents position rather than actual motion. For part of the energy of absorbed heat is spent in pulling asunder the molecules of the body under the attractive force which binds them together (Art. 73), and thus a store of energy of position is laid up, which disappears again after the body is cooled.

Atomic or Chemical Separation.

111. (E.) The two previous varieties of energy may be viewed as associated with molecules rather than with atoms, and with the force of cohesion rather than with that of chemical affinity. Proceeding now to atomic force, we have a species of energy of position due to the

separation of different atoms under the strong chemical attraction they have for one another. Thus, when we possess coal or carbon and also oxygen in a state of separation from one another, we are in possession of a source of energy which may be called that of chemical separation.

Electrical Separation.

112. (F.) The attraction which heterogeneous atoms possess for one another, sometimes, however, gives rise to a species of energy which manifests itself in a very peculiar form, and appears as electrical separation, which is thus another form of energy of position.

Electricity in Motion.

113. (G.) But we have another species of energy connected with electricity, for we have that due to electricity in motion, or in other words, an electric current which probably represents some form of actual motion.

Radiant Energy.

114. (H.) It is well known that there is no ordinary matter, or at least hardly any, between the sun and the earth, and yet we have a kind of energy

which we may call radiant energy, which proceeds to us from the sun, and proceeds also with a definite, though very great velocity, taking about eight minutes to perform its journey. Now, this radiant energy is known to consist of the vibrations of an elastic medium pervading all space, which is called ether, or the *ethereal medium*. Inasmuch, therefore, as it consists of vibrations, it partakes of the character of pendulum motion, that is to say, the energy of any ethereal particle is alternately that of position and that of actual motion.

Law of Conservation.

115. Having thus endeavoured, provisionally at least, to catalogue our various energies, we are in a position to state more definitely what is meant by the conservation of energy. For this purpose, let us take the universe as a whole, or, if this be too large, let us conceive, if possible, a small portion of it to be isolated from the rest, as far as force or energy is concerned, forming a sort of microcosm, to which we may conveniently direct our attention.

This portion, then, neither parts with any of its energy to the universe beyond, nor receives any from it. Such an isolation is, of course, unnatural and impossible, but it is conceivable, and will, at least, tend to concentrate our thoughts. Now, whether we regard the great universe,

STATEMENT OF THE LAW OF CONSERVATION. 83

or this small microcosm, the principle of the conservation of energy asserts that the sum of all the various energies is a constant quantity, that is to say, adopting the language of Algebra—

$$(A) + (B) + (C) + (D) + (E) + (F) + (G) + (H) = \text{a constant quantity.}$$

116. This does not mean, of course, that (A) is constant in itself, or any other of the left-hand members of this equation, for, in truth, they are always changing about into each other—now, some visible energy being changed into heat or electricity; and, anon, some heat or electricity being changed back again into visible energy—but it only means that the sum of all the energies taken together is constant. We have, in fact, in the left hand, eight variable quantities, and we only assert that their sum is constant, not by any means that they are constant themselves.

117. Now, what evidence have we for this assertion? It may be replied that we have the strongest possible evidence which the nature of the case admits of. The assertion is, in truth, a peculiar one—peculiar in its magnitude, in its universality, in the subtle nature of the agents with which it deals. If true, its truth certainly cannot be proved after the manner in which we prove a proposition in Euclid. Nor does it even admit of a proof so rigid as that of the somewhat analogous principle of the conservation of matter, for in chemistry we may

confine the products of our chemical combination so completely as to prove, beyond a doubt, that no heavy matter passes out of existence that—when coal, for instance, burns in oxygen gas—what we have is merely a change of condition. But we cannot so easily prove that no energy is destroyed in this combination, and that the only result is a change from the energy of chemical separation into that of absorbed heat, for during the process it is impossible to isolate the energy—do what we may, some of it will escape into the room in which we perform the experiment; some of it will, no doubt, escape through the window, while a little will leave the earth altogether, and go out into space. All that we can do in such a case is to estimate, as completely as possible, how much energy has gone away, since we cannot possibly prevent its going. But this is an operation involving great acquaintance with the laws of energy, and very great exactness of observation: in fine, our readers will at once perceive that it is much more difficult to prove the truth of the conservation of energy than that of the conservation of matter.

118. But if it be difficult to prove our principle in the most rigorous manner, we are yet able to give the strongest possible indirect evidence of its truth.

Our readers are no doubt familiar with a method which Euclid frequently adopts in proving his propositions. Starting with the supposition that they are not true, and reasoning upon this hypothesis, he comes to an absurd conclusion—hence he concludes that they are true. Now, we may adopt a method somewhat similar with regard to our principle, only instead of supposing it untrue, let us suppose it true. It may then be shown that, if it be true, under certain test conditions we ought to obtain certain results—for instance, if we increase the pressure, we ought to lower the freezing point of water. Well, we make the experiment, and find that, in point of fact, the freezing point of water is lowered by increasing the pressure, and we have thus derived an argument in favour of the conservation of energy.

119. Or again, if the laws of energy are true, it may be shown that, whenever a substance contracts when heated, it will become colder instead of hotter by compression. Now, we know that ice-cold water, or water just a little above its freezing point, contracts instead of expanding up to $4°$ C.; and Sir William Thomson has found, by experiment, that water at this temperature is cooled instead of heated by sudden compression. India-rubber is another instance of this relation between these two properties, for if we stretch a string of india-rubber it gets hotter instead of colder, that is to say, its temperature rises by extension, and gets lower by contraction; and again, if we heat the string, we find that it contracts in length instead of expanding like other substances as its temperature increases.

120. Numberless instances occur in which we are

enabled to predict what will happen by assuming the truth of the laws of energy; in other words, these laws are proved to be true in all cases where we can put them to the test of rigorous experiment, and probably we can have no better proof than this of the truth of such a principle. We shall therefore proceed upon the assumption that the conservation of energy holds true in all cases, and give our readers a list of the various transmutations of this subtle agent as it goes backwards and forwards from one abode to another, making, meanwhile, sundry remarks that may tend, we trust, to convince our readers of the truth of our assumption.

CHAPTER IV.

TRANSMUTATIONS OF ENERGY.

Energy of Visible Motion.

121. LET us begin our list of transmutations with the energy of visible motion. This is changed into *energy of position* when a stone is projected upwards above the earth, or, to take a case precisely similar, when a planet or a comet goes from perihelion, or its position nearest the sun, to aphelion, or its position furthest from the sun. We thus see why a heavenly body should move fastest at perihelion, and slowest at aphelion. If, however, a planet were to move round the sun in an orbit exactly circular, its velocity would be the same at all the various points of this orbit, because there would be no change in its distance from the centre of attraction, and therefore no transmutation of energy.

122. We have already (Arts. 108, 109) said that the energy in an oscillating or vibrating body is alternately that of actual motion, and that of position. In this respect, therefore, a pendulum is similar to a comet or heavenly body with an elliptical orbit. Nevertheless the

change of energy is generally more complete in a pendulum or vibrating body than it is in a heavenly body; for in a pendulum, when at its lowest point, the energy is entirely that of actual motion, while at its upper point it is entirely that of position. Now, in a heavenly body we have only a lessening, but not an entire destruction, of the velocity, as the body passes from perihelion to aphelion—that is to say, we have only a partial conversion of the one kind of energy into the other.

123. Let us next consider the change of actual visible energy into *absorbed heat*. This takes place in all cases of friction, percussion, and resistance. In friction, for instance, we have the conversion of work or energy into heat, which is here produced through the rubbing of surfaces against each other; and Davy has shown that two pieces of ice, both colder than the freezing point, may be melted by friction. In percussion, again, we have the energy of the blow converted into heat; while, in the case of a meteor or cannon ball passing through the air with great velocity, we have the loss of energy of the meteor or cannon ball through its contact with the air, and at the same time the production of heat on account of this resistance.

The resistance need not be atmospheric, for we may set the cannon ball to pierce through wooden planks or through sand, and there will equally be a production of heat on account of the resistance offered by the wooden planks or by the sand to the motion of the ball. We may even generalize still further, and assert that whenever the visible momentum of a body is transferred to a larger mass, there is at the same time the conversion of visible energy into heat.

124. A little explanation will be required to make this point clear.

The third law of motion tells us that action and reaction are equal and opposite, so that when two bodies come into collision the forces at work generate equal and opposite quantities of momentum. We shall best see the meaning of this law by a numerical example, bearing in mind that momentum means the product of mass into velocity.

For instance, let us suppose that an inelastic body of mass 10 and velocity 20 strikes directly another inelastic body of mass 15 and velocity 15, the direction of both motions being the same.

Now, it is well known that the united mass will, after impact, be moving with the velocity 17. What, then, has been the influence of the forces developed by collision? The body of greater velocity had before impact a momentum $10 \times 20 = 200$, while its momentum after impact is only $10 \times 17 = 170$; it has therefore suffered a loss of 30 units as regards momentum, or we may consider that a momentum of 30 units has been impressed upon it in an opposite direction to its previous motion.

On the other hand, the body of smaller velocity had before impact a momentum $15 \times 15 = 225$, while after impact it has $15 \times 17 = 255$ units, so that its momentum has been increased by 30 units in its previous direction.

The force of impact has therefore generated 30 units of momentum in two opposite directions, so that, taking account of direction, the momentum of the system is the same before and after impact ; for before impact we had a momentum of $10 \times 20 + 15 \times 15 = 425$, while after it we have the united mass 25 moving with the velocity 17, giving the momentum 425 as before.

125. But while the momentum is the same before and after impact, the visible energy of the moving mass is undoubtedly less after impact than before it. To see this we have only to turn to the expression of Art. 28, from which we find that the energy before impact was as follows:—Energy in kilogrammetres $= \dfrac{m\,v^2}{19\cdot 6} = \dfrac{10 \times 20^2 + 15 \times 15^2}{19\cdot 6} = 376$ nearly; while that after impact $= \dfrac{25 \times 17^2}{19\cdot 6} = 368$ nearly.

126. The loss of energy will be still more manifest if we suppose an inelastic body in motion to strike against a similar body at rest. Thus if we have a body of mass 20 and velocity 20 striking against one of equal mass, but at rest, the velocity of the double mass after impact will obviously be only 10; but, as regards energy, that before impact will be $\dfrac{20 \times 20^2}{19\cdot 6} = \dfrac{8000}{19\cdot 6}$ while that after

impact will be $\dfrac{40 \times 10^3}{19 \cdot 6} = \dfrac{4000}{19 \cdot 6}$ or only half the former.

127. Thus there is in all such cases an apparent loss of visible energy, while at the same time there is the production of heat on account of the blow which takes place. If, however, the substances that come together be perfectly elastic (which no substance is), the visible energy after impact will be the same as that before, and in this case there will be no conversion into heat. This, however, is an extreme supposition, and inasmuch as no substance is perfectly elastic, we have in all cases of collision a greater or less conversion of visible motion into heat.

128. We have spoken (Art. 122) about the change of energy in an oscillating or vibrating body, as if it were entirely one of actual energy into energy of position, and the reverse.

But even here, in each oscillation or vibration, there is a greater or less conversion of visible energy into heat. Let us, for instance, take a pendulum, and, in order to make the circumstances as favourable as possible, let it swing on a knife edge, and in vacuo; in this case there will be a slight but constant friction of the knife edge against the plane on which it rests, and though the pendulum may continue to swing for hours, yet it will ultimately come to rest.

And, again, it is impossible to make a vacuum so perfect that there is absolutely no air surrounding the pendulum, so that part of the motion of the pendulum will always be carried off by the residual air of the vacuum in which it swings.

129. Now, something similar happens in that vibratory motion which constitutes sound. Thus, when a bell is in vibration, part of the energy of the vibration is carried off by the surrounding air, and it is in virtue of this that we hear the sound of the bell; but, even if there were no air, the bell would not go on vibrating for ever. For there is in all bodies a greater or less amount of internal viscosity, a property which prevents perfect freedom of vibration, and which ultimately converts vibrations into heat.

A vibrating bell is thus very much in the same position as an oscillating pendulum, for in both part of the energy is given off to the air, and in both there is unavoidable friction—in the one taking the shape of internal viscosity, and in the other that of friction of the knife edge against the plane on which it rests.

130. In both these cases, too, that portion of the energy which goes into the air takes ultimately the shape of heat. The oscillating pendulum communicates a motion to the air, and this motion ultimately heats the air. The vibrating bell, or musical instrument, in like manner communicates part of its energy to the air. This communicated energy first of all moves through the air with the well-known velocity of sound, but during its progress it, too, no doubt becomes partly converted into heat. Ultimately, it is transmitted by the air to other bodies,

and by means of their internal viscosity is sooner or later converted into heat. Thus we see that heat is the form of energy, into which all visible terrestrial motion, whether it be rectilinear, or oscillatory, or vibratory, is ultimately changed.

131. In the case of a body in visible rectilinear motion on the earth's surface, this change takes place very soon—if the motion be rotatory, such as that of a heavy revolving top, it may, perhaps, continue longer before it is ultimately stopped, by means of the surrounding air, and by friction of the pivot; if it be oscillatory, as in the pendulum, or vibratory, as in a musical instrument, we have seen that the air and internal friction are at work, in one shape or another, to carry it off, and will ultimately succeed in converting it into heat.

132. But, it may be said, why consider a body moving on the earth's surface? why not consider the motion of the earth itself? Will this also ultimately take the shape of heat?

No doubt it is more difficult to trace the conversion in such a case, inasmuch as it is not proceeding at a sensible rate before our eyes. In other words, the very conditions that make the earth habitable, and a fit abode for intelligent beings like ourselves, are those which unfit us to perceive this conversion of energy in the case of the earth. Yet we are not without indications that it is actually taking place. For the purpose of exhibiting these, we may divide the earth's motion into two—a motion of rotation, and one of revolution.

133. Now, with regard to the earth's rotation, the conversion of the visible energy of this motion into heat is already well recognized. To understand this we have only to study the nature of the moon's action upon the fluid portions of our globe. In the following diagram (Fig. 11) we have an exaggerated representation of this, by which we see that the spherical earth is converted

Fig. 11.

into an elongated oval, of which one extremity always points to the moon. The solid body of the earth itself revolves as usual, but, nevertheless, this fluid protuberance remains always pointing towards the moon, as we see in the figure, and hence the earth rubs against the protuberance as it revolves. The friction produced by this action tends evidently to lessen the rotatory energy of the earth—in other words, it acts like a break—and we have, just as by a break-wheel, the conversion of visible energy into heat. This was first recognized by Mayer and J. Thomson.

134. But while there can be no doubt about the fact of such a conversion going on, the only question is regarding

its rate of progress, and the time required before it can cause a perceptible impression upon the rotative energy of the earth.

Now, it is believed by astronomers that they have detected evidence of such a change, for our knowledge of the motions of the sun and moon has become so exact, that not only can we carry forward our calculations so as to predict an eclipse, but also carry them backwards, and thus fix the dates and even the very details of the ancient historical eclipses.

If, however, between those times and the present, the earth has lost a little rotative energy on account of this peculiar action of the moon, then it is evident that the calculated circumstances of the ancient total eclipse will not quite agree with those actually recorded; and by a comparison of this nature it is believed that we have detected a very slight falling off in the rotative energy of our earth. If we carry out the argument, we shall be driven to the conclusion that the rotative energy of our globe will, on account of the moon's action, always get less and less, until things are brought into such a state that the rotation comes to be performed in the same time as the revolution of the moon, so that then the same portion of the terrestrial surface being always presented to the moon, it is evident that there will be no effort made by the solid substance of the earth, to glide from under the fluid protuberance, and there will in consequence be no friction, and no further loss of energy.

135. If the fate of the earth be ultimately to turn the same face always to the moon, we have abundant evidence that this very fate has long since overtaken the moon herself. Indeed, the much stronger effect of our earth upon the moon has produced this result, probably, even in those remote periods when the moon was chiefly fluid; and it is a fact well known, not merely to astronomers, but to all of us, that the moon nowadays turns always the same face to the earth.* No doubt this fate has long since overtaken the satellites of Jupiter, Saturn, and the other large planets; and there are independent indications that, at least in the case of Jupiter, the satellites turn always the same face to their primary.

136. To come now to the energy of revolution of the earth, in her orbit round the sun, we cannot help believing that there is a material medium of some kind between the sun and the earth; indeed, the undulatory theory of light requires this belief. But if we believe in such a medium, it is difficult to imagine that its presence will not ultimately diminish the motion of revolution of the earth in her orbit; indeed, there is a strong scientific probability, if not an absolute certainty, that such will be the case. There is even some reason to think that the energy of a comet of small period, called Encke's comet, is gradually being stopped from this cause; in fine, there can be hardly any doubt that the cause is really in operation,

* This explanation was first given by Professors Thomson and Tait in their Natural Philosophy, and by Dr. Frankland in a lecture at the Royal Institution of London.

and will ultimately affect the motions of the planets and other heavenly bodies, even although its rate of action may be so slow that we are not able to detect it.

We may perhaps generalize by saying, that wherever in the universe there is a differential motion, that is to say, a motion of one part of it towards or from another, then, in virtue of the subtle medium, or cement, that binds the various parts of the universe together, this motion is not unattended by something like friction, in virtue of which the differential motion will ultimately disappear, while the loss of energy caused by its disappearance will assume the form of heat.

137. There are, indeed, obscure intimations that a conversion of this kind is not improbably taking place in the solar system; for, in the sun himself, we have the matter near the equator, by virtue of the rotation of our luminary, carried alternately towards and from the various planets. Now, it would seem that the sun-spots, or atmospheric disturbances of the sun, affect particularly his equatorial regions, and have likewise a tendency to attain their maximum size in that position, which is as far away as possible from the influential planets, such as Mercury or Venus;* so that if Venus, for instance, were between the earth and the sun, there would be few sun-spots in the middle of the sun's disc, because that would be the part of the sun nearest Venus.

* *See* De La Rue, Stewart, and Loewy's researches on Solar Physics.

H

But if the planets influence sun-spots, the action is no doubt reciprocal, and we have much reason to believe that sun-spots influence, not only the magnetism, but also the meteorology of our earth, so that there are most displays of the Aurora Borealis, as well as most cyclones, in those years when there are most sun-spots.* Is it not then possible that, in these strange, mysterious phenomena, we see traces of the machinery by means of which the differential motion of the solar system is gradually being changed into heat?

138. We have thus seen that visible energy of actual motion is not unfrequently changed into visible energy of position, and that it is also very often transformed into absorbed heat. We have now to state that it may likewise be transformed into *electrical separation*. Thus, when an ordinary electrical machine is in action, considerable labour is spent in turning the handle; it is, in truth, harder to turn than if no electricity were being produced— in other words, part of the energy which is spent upon the machine goes to the production of electrical separation. There are other ways of generating electricity besides the frictional method. If, for instance, we bring an insulated conducting plate near the prime conductor of the electrical machine, yet not near enough to cause a spark to pass, and if we then touch the insulated plate, we shall find it, after contact, to be charged with an electricity the oppo-

* See the Magnetic Researches of Sir E. Sabine, also C. Meldrum on the Periodicity of Cyclones.

site of that in the machine; we may then remove it and make use of this electricity

It requires a little thought to see what labour we have spent in this process. We must bear in mind that, by touching the plate, we have carried off the electricity of the same name as that of the machine, so that, after touching the insulated plate it is more strongly attracted to the conductor than it was before. When we begin to remove it, therefore, it will cost us an effort to do so, and the mechanical energy which we spend in removing it will account for the energy of electrical separation which we then obtain.

139. We may thus make use of a small nucleus of electricity, to assist us in procuring an unlimited supply, for in the above process the electricity of the prime conductor remains unaltered, and we may repeat the operation as often as we like, and gather together a very large quantity of electricity, without finally altering the electricity of the prime conductor, but not, however, without the expenditure of an equivalent amount of energy, in the shape of actual work.

140. While, as we have seen, there is a tendency in all motion to be changed into heat, there is one instance where it is, in the first place at least, changed into *a current of electricity.* We allude to the case where a conducting substance moves in the presence of an electric current, or of a magnet.

In Art. 104 we found that if one coil connected with a

battery were quickly moved into the presence of another coil connected with a galvanometer, an induced current would be generated in the latter coil, and would affect the galvanometer, its direction being the reverse of that passing in the other. Now, an electric current implies energy, and we may therefore conclude that some other form of energy must be spent, or disappear, in order to produce the current which is generated in the coil attached to the galvanometer.

Again, we learn from Art. 100 that two currents going in opposite directions repel one another. The current generated in the coil attached to the galvanometer or secondary current will, therefore, repel the primary current, which is moving towards it; this repulsion will either cause a stoppage of motion, or render necessary the expenditure of energy, in order to keep up the motion of this moving coil. We thus find that two phenomena occur simultaneously. In the first place, there is the production of energy in the secondary coil, in the shape of a current opposite in direction to that of the primary coil; in the next case, owing to the repulsion between this induced current and the primary current, there is a stoppage or disappearance of the energy of actual motion of the moving coil. We have, in fact, the creation of one species of energy, and at the same time the disappearance of another, and thus we see that the law of conservation is by no means broken.

141. We see also the necessary connection between the

two electrical laws described in Arts. 100 and 104. Indeed, had these laws been other than what they are, the principle of conservation of energy would have been broken.

For instance, had the induced current in the case now mentioned been in the same direction as that of the primary, the two currents would have attracted each other, and thus there would have been the creation of a secondary current, implying energy, in the coil attached to the galvanometer, along with an increase of the visible energy of motion of the primary current—that is to say, instead of the creation of one kind of energy, accompanied with the disappearance of another, we should have had the simultaneous creation of both; and thus the law of conservation of energy would have been broken.

We thus see that the principle of conservation enables us to deduce the one electrical law from the other, and this is one of the many instances which strengthen our belief in the truth of the great principle for which we are contending.

142. Let us next consider what will take place if we cause the primary current to move from the secondary coil instead of towards it.

In this case we know, from Art. 104, that the induced current will be in the same direction as the primary, while we are told by Art. 100 that the two currents will now attract each other. The tendency of this attraction will be to stop the motion of the primary current from the secondary one, or, in other words, there will be a disappearance of the energy of visible motion, while at the same time there is the production of a current. In both cases, therefore, one form of energy disappears while another takes its place, and in both there will be a very perceptible resistance experienced in moving the primary coil, whether towards the secondary or from it. Work will, in fact, have to be spent in both operations, and the outcome of this work or energy will be the production of a current in the first place, and of heat in the second; for we learn from Art. 98 that when a current passes along a wire its energy is generally spent in heating the wire.

We have thus two phenomena occurring together. In the first place, in moving a current of electricity to and from a coil of wire, or any other conductor, or (which is the same thing, since action and reaction are equal and opposite) in moving a coil of wire or any other conductor to and from a current of electricity, a sense of resistance will be experienced, and energy will have to be spent upon the process; in the second place, an electrical current will be generated in the conductor, and the conductor will be heated in consequence.

143. The result will be rendered very prominent if we cause a metallic top, in rapid rotation, to spin near two iron poles, which, by means of the battery, we can suddenly convert into the poles of a powerful electro-

magnet. When this change is made, and the poles become magnetic, the motion of the top is very speedily brought to rest, just as if it had to encounter a species of invisible friction. This curious result can easily be explained. We have seen from Art. 101 that a magnet resembles an assemblage of electric currents, and in the metallic top we have a conductor alternately approaching these currents and receding from them; and hence, according to what has been said, we shall have a series of secondary currents produced in the conducting top which will stop its motion, and which will ultimately take the shape of heat. In other words, the visible energy of the top will be changed into heat just as truly as if it were stopped by ordinary friction.

144. The electricity induced in a metallic conductor, moved in the presence of a powerful magnet, has received the name of Magneto-Electricity; and Dr. Joule has made use of it as a convenient means of enabling him to determine the mechanical equivalent of heat, for it is into heat that the energy of motion of the conductor is ultimately transformed. But, besides all this, these currents form, perhaps, the very best means of obtaining electricity; and recently very powerful machines have been constructed by Wilde and others with this view.

145. These machines, when large, are worked by a steam-engine, and their mode of operation is as follows:— The nucleus of the machine is a system of powerful permanent steel magnets, and a conducting coil is made

to revolve rapidly in presence of these magnets. The current produced by this moving coil is then used in order to produce an extremely powerful electro-magnet, and finally a coil is made to move with great rapidity in presence of this powerful electro-magnet, thus causing induced currents of vast strength. So powerful are these currents, that when used to produce the electric light, small print may be read on a dark night at the distance of two miles from the scene of operation !

It thus appears that in this machine a double use is made of magneto-electricity. Starting with a nucleus of permanent magnetism, the magneto-electric currents are used, in the first instance, to form a powerful electro-magnet much stronger than the first, and this powerful electro-magnet is again made use of in the same way as, the first, in order to give, by means of magneto-electricity, an induced current of very great strength.

146. There is, moreover, a very great likeness between a magneto-electric machine like that of Wilde's for generating electric currents, and the one which generates statical electricity by means of the method already described Art. 139. In both cases advantage is taken of a nucleus, for in the magneto-electric machine we have the molecular currents of a set of permanent magnets, which are made the means of generating enormous electric currents without any permanent alteration to themselves, yet not without the expenditure of work.

Again, in an induction machine for generating statical

electricity, we have an electric nucleus, such as we have supposed to reside in the prime conductor of a machine; and advantage may be taken, as we have seen, of this nucleus in order to generate a vast quantity of statical electricity, without any permanent alteration of the nucleus, but not without the expenditure of work.

147. We have now seen under what conditions the visible energy of actual motion may be changed—1stly, into energy of position; 2ndly, into the two energies which embrace absorbed heat; 3rdly, into electrical separation; and finally into electricity in motion. As far as we know, visible energy cannot directly be transformed into chemical separation, or into radiant energy.

Visible Energy of Position.

148. Having thus exhausted the transmutations of the energy of visible motion, we next turn to that of position, and find that it is transmuted into motion, but not immediately into any other form of energy; we may, therefore, dismiss this variety at once from our consideration.

Absorbed Heat.

149. Coming now to these two forms of energy which embrace *absorbed heat*, we find that this may be converted into (A) or *actual visible energy* in the case of the steam-engine, the air-engine, and all varieties of heat engines. In the steam-engine, for instance, part of the

heat which passes through it disappears as heat, utterly and absolutely, to reappear as mechanical effect. There is, however, one condition which must be rigidly fulfilled, whenever heat is changed into mechanical effect—there must be a difference of temperature, and *heat will only be changed into work, while it passes from a body of high temperature to one of low.*

Carnot, the celebrated French physicist, has ingeniously likened the mechanical power of heat to that of water; for just as you can get no work out of heat unless there be a flow of heat from a higher temperature level to a lower, so neither can you get work out of water unless it be falling from a higher level to a lower.

150. If we reflect that heat is essentially distributive in its nature, we shall soon perceive the reason for this peculiar law; for, in virtue of its nature, heat is always rushing from a body of high temperature to one of low, and if left to itself it would distribute itself equally amongst all bodies, so that they would ultimately become of the same temperature. Now, if we are to coax work out of heat, we must humour its nature, for it may be compared to a pack of schoolboys, who are always ready to run with sufficient violence out of the schoolroom into the open fields, but who have frequently to be dragged back with a very considerable expenditure of energy. So heat will not allow itself to be confined, but will resist any attempt to accumulate it into a limited space. Work cannot, therefore, be gained by

such an operation, but must, on the contrary, be spent upon the process.

151. Let us now for a moment consider the case of an enclosure in which everything is of the same temperature. Here we have a dull dead level of heat, out of which it will be impossible to obtain the faintest semblance of work. The temperature may even be high, and there may be immense stores of heat energy in the enclosure, but not a trace of this is available in the shape of work. Taking up Carnot's comparison, the water has already fallen to the same level, and lies there without any power of doing useful work—dead, in a sense, as far as visible energy is concerned.

152. We thus perceive that, firstly, we can get work out of heat when it passes from a higher to a lower temperature, but that, secondly, we must spend work upon it in order to make it pass from a lower temperature to a higher one; and that, thirdly and finally, nothing in the shape of work can be got out of heat which is all at the same temperature level.

What we have now said enables us to realize the conditions under which all heat engines work. The essential point about such engines is, not the possession of a cylinder, or piston, or fly wheels, or valves, but the possession of two chambers, one of high and the other of low temperature, while it performs work in the process of carrying heat from the chamber of high to that of low temperature.

Let us take, for example, the low-pressure engine. Here we have the boiler or chamber of high, and the condenser or chamber of low, temperature, and the engine works while heat is being carried from the boiler to the condenser—never while it is being carried from the condenser to the boiler.

In like manner in the locomotive we have the steam generated at a high temperature and pressure, and cooled by injection into the atmosphere.

153. But, leaving formal engines, let us take an ordinary fire, which plays in truth the part of an engine, as far as energy is concerned. We have here the cold air streaming in over the floor of the room, and rushing into the fire, to be there united with carbon, while the rarefied product is carried up the chimney. Dismissing from our thoughts at present the process of combustion, except as a means of supplying heat, we see that there is a continual in-draught of cold air, which is heated by the fire, and then sent to mingle with the air above. Heat is, in fact, distributed by this means, or carried from a body of high temperature, i.e. the fire, to a body of low temperature, i.e. the outer air, and in this process of distribution mechanical effect is obtained in the up-rush of air through the chimney with considerable velocity.

154. Our own earth is another instance of such an engine, having the equatorial regions as its boiler, and the polar regions as its condensers; for, at the equator, the air is heated by the direct rays

of the sun, and we have there an ascending current of air, up a chimney as it were, the place of which is supplied by an in-draught of colder air along the ground or floor of the world, from the poles on both sides. Thus the heated air makes its way from the equator to the poles in the upper regions of the atmosphere, while the cold air makes its way from the poles to the equator along the lower regions. Very often, too, aqueous vapour as well as air is carried up by means of the sun's heat to the upper and colder atmospheric regions, and there deposited in the shape of rain, or hail, or snow, which ultimately finds its way back again to the earth, often displaying in its passage immense mechanical energy. Indeed, the mariner who hoists his sail, and the miller who grinds his corn (whether he use the force of the wind or that of running water), are both dependent upon this great earth-engine, which is constantly at work producing mechanical effect, but always in the act of carrying heat from its hotter to its colder regions.

155. Now, if it be essential to an engine to have two chambers, one hot and one cold, it is equally important that there should be a considerable temperature difference between the two.

If Nature insists upon a difference before she will give us work, we shall not be able to pacify her, or to meet her requirements by making this difference as small as possible. And hence, *cæteris paribus*, we shall obtain a greater proportion of work out of a certain amount of heat passing through our engine when the temperature difference between its boiler and condenser is as great as possible. In a steam-engine this difference cannot be very great, because if the water of the boiler were at a very high temperature the pressure of its steam would become dangerous; but in an air-engine, or engine that heats and cools air, the temperature difference may be much larger. There are, however, practical inconveniences in engines for which the temperature of the boiler is very high, and it is possible that these may prove so formidable as to turn the scale against such engines, although in theory they ought to be very economical.

156. The principles now stated have been employed by Professor J. Thomson, in his suggestion that the application of pressure would be found to lower the freezing point of water; and the truth of this suggestion was afterwards proved by Professor Sir W. Thomson. The following was the reasoning employed by the former:—

Suppose that we have a chamber kept constantly at the temperature 0° C., or the melting point of ice, and that we have a cylinder, of which the sectional area is one square metre, filled one metre in height with water, that is to say, containing one cubic metre of water. Suppose, next, that a well-fitting piston is placed above the surface of the water in this cylinder, and that a considerable weight is placed upon the piston. Let us now take the cylinder, water and all, and carry it into another room, of which the temperature is just a trifle lower. In course of time the water will freeze, and, as it expands in freezing, it will push up the piston and weight about $\frac{1}{12}$ths of a metre; and we may suppose that the piston is kept fastened in this position by means of a peg. Now carry back the machine into the first room, and in the course of time the ice will be melted, and we shall have water once more in the cylinder, but there will now be a void space of $\frac{1}{12}$ths of a metre between the piston and the surface. We have thus acquired a certain amount of energy of position, and we have only to pull out the peg, and allow the piston with its weight to fall down through the vacant space, in order to utilize this energy, after which the arrangement is ready to start afresh. Again, if the weight be very great, the energy thus gained will be very great; in fact, the energy will vary with the weight. In fine, the arrangement now described is a veritable heat engine, of which the chamber at 0° C. corresponds to the boiler, and the other chamber a trifle lower in temperature to the condenser, while the amount of work we get out of the engine—or, in other words, its efficiency—will depend upon the weight which is raised through the space of $\frac{1}{12}$ths of a metre, so that, by increasing this weight without limit, we may increase the efficiency of our engine without limit. It would thus at first sight appear that by this device of having two chambers, one at 0° C., and the other a trifle lower, we can get any amount of work out of our water engine; and that, consequently, we have managed to overcome

Nature. But here Thomson's law comes into operation, showing that we cannot overcome Nature by any such device, but that if we have a large weight upon our piston, we must have a proportionally large difference of temperature between our two chambers—that is to say, the freezing point of water, under great pressure, will be lower in temperature than its freezing point, if the pressure upon it be only small.

Before leaving this subject we must call upon our readers to realize what takes place in all heat engines. It is not merely that heat produces mechanical effect, but that *a given quantity of heat absolutely passes out of existence as heat in producing its equivalent of work.* If, therefore, we could measure the mere heat produced in an engine by the burning of a ton of coals, we should find it to be less when the engine was doing work than when it was at rest.

In like manner, when a gas expands suddenly its temperature falls, because a certain amount of its heat passes out of existence in the act of producing mechanical effect.

157. We have thus endeavoured to show under what conditions absorbed heat may be converted into mechanical effect. This absorbed heat embraces (Art. 110) two varieties of energy, one of these being molecular motion, and the other molecular energy of position.

Let us now, therefore, endeavour to ascertain under what circumstances the one of these varieties may be changed into the other. It is well known that it takes a good deal of heat to convert a kilogramme of ice into water, and that when the ice is melted the temperature of the water is not perceptibly higher than that of the ice. It is equally well known that it takes a great deal of heat to convert a kilogramme of boiling water into steam, and that when the transformation is accomplished, the steam produced is not perceptibly hotter than the boiling water. In such cases the heat is said to become latent.

Now, in both these cases, but more obviously in the last, we may suppose that the heat has not had its usual office to perform, but that, instead of increasing the motion of the molecules of water, it has spent its energy in tearing them asunder from each other, against the force of cohesion which binds them together.

Indeed, we know as a matter of fact that the force of cohesion which is perceptible in boiling water is apparently absent from steam, or the vapour of water, because its molecules are too remote from one another to allow of this force being appreciable. We may, therefore, suppose that a large part, at least, of the heat necessary to convert boiling water into steam is spent in doing work against molecular forces.

When the steam is once more condensed into hot water, the heat thus spent reassumes the form of molecular motion, and the consequence is that we require to take away somehow all the latent heat of a kilogramme of steam before we can convert it into boiling water. In fact, if it is difficult and tedious to convert water into steam, it is difficult and tedious to convert steam into water.

158. Besides the case now mentioned, there are other instances in which, no doubt, molecular separation becomes gradually changed into heat motion. Thus, when a piece of glass has been suddenly cooled, its particles have not had time to acquire their proper position, and the consequence is that the whole structure is thrown into a state of constraint. In the course of time such bodies tend to assume a more stable state, and their particles gradually come closer together.

It is owing to this cause that the bulb of a thermometer recently blown gradually contracts, and it is no doubt owing to the same cause that a Prince Rupert's drop, formed by dropping melted glass into water, when broken, falls into powder with a kind of explosion. It seems probable that in all such cases these changes are attended with heat, and that they denote the conversion of the energy of molecular separation into that of molecular motion.

159. Having thus examined the transmutations of (C) into (D), and of (D) back again into (C), let us now proceed with our list, and see under what circumstances absorbed heat is changed into *chemical separation*.

It is well known that when certain bodies are heated, they are decomposed; for instance, if limestone or carbonate of lime be heated, it is decomposed, the carbonic acid being given out in the shape of gas, while quicklime remains behind. Now, heat is consumed in this process, that is to say, a certain amount of heat energy absolutely passes out of existence *as heat* and is changed into the energy of chemical separation. Again, if the lime so obtained be exposed, under certain circumstances, to an atmosphere of carbonic acid, it will gradually become changed into carbonate of lime; and in this change (which is a gradual one) we may feel assured that the energy of chemical separation is once more converted into the energy of heat, although we may not perceive any increment of temperature, on account of the slow nature of the process.

At very high temperatures it is possible that most compounds are decomposed, and the temperature at which this takes place, for any compound, has been termed its *temperature of disassociation*.

160. Heat energy is changed into *electrical separation* when tourmalines and certain other crystals are heated.

Let us take, for instance, a crystal of tourmaline and raise its temperature, and we shall find one end positively, and the other negatively, electrified. Again, let us take the same crystal, and suddenly cool it, and we shall find an electrification of the opposite kind to the former, so that the end of the axis, which was then positive, will now be negative. Now, this separation of the electricities denotes energy; and we have, therefore, in such crystals a case where the energy of heat has been changed into that of electrical separation. In other words, a certain amount of heat has passed out of existence *as heat*, while in its place a certain amount of electrical separation has been obtained.

161. Let us next see under what circumstances heat is changed into *electricity in motion*. This transmutation takes place in thermo-electricity.

Suppose, for instance, that we have a bar of copper or antimony, say copper, soldered to a bar of bismuth, as in Fig. 12. Let us now heat one of the junctions, while the other remains cool. It will be found that a current of positive electricity circulates round the bar, in the direction of the arrow-head, going from the bismuth to the copper across the heated junction, the existence of which may be detected by means of a compass needle, as we see in the figure.

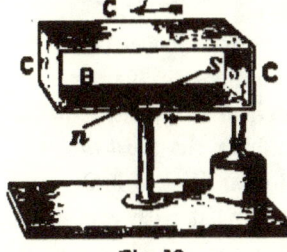

Fig. 12.

Here, then, we have a case in which heat energy goes out of existence, and is converted into that of an electric current, and we may even arrange matters so as to make, on this principle, an instrument which shall be an extremely delicate test of the existence of heat.

By having a number of junctions of bismuth and

antimony, as in Fig. 13, and heating the upper set, while the lower remain cool, we get a strong current going from the bismuth to the antimony across the heated junctions, and we may pass the current so produced round the wire of a galvanometer, and thus, by increasing the number of our junctions, and also by using a very delicate galvanometer, we may get a very perceptible effect for the smallest heating of the upper junctions. This arrangement is called the *thermopile*, and, in conjunction with the reflecting galvanometer, it affords the most delicate means known for detecting small quantities of heat.

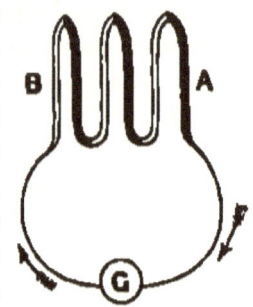

Fig. 13.

162. The last transmutation on our list with respect to absorbed heat is that in which this species of energy is transformed into *radiant light and heat*. This takes place whenever a hot body cools in an open space—the sun, for instance, parts with a large quantity of his heat in this way; and it is due, in part at least, to this process that a hot body cools in air, and wholly to it that such a body cools in vacuo. It is, moreover, due to the penetration of our eye by radiant energy that we are able to see hot bodies, and thus the very fact that we see them implies that they are parting with their heat.

Radiant energy moves through space with the enormous velocity of 188,000 miles in one second. It takes about eight minutes to come from the sun to our earth, so that if our luminary were to be suddenly extinguished, we should have eight minutes, respite before the catastrophe overtook us. Besides the rays that affect the eye, there are others which we cannot see, and which may therefore be termed dark rays. A body, for instance, may not be hot enough to be self-luminous, and yet it may be rapidly cooling and changing its heat into radiant energy, which is given off by the body, even although neither the eye nor the touch may be competent to detect it. It may nevertheless be detected by the thermopile, which was described in Art. 161. We thus see how strong is the likeness between a heated body and a sounding one. For just as a sounding body gives out part of its sound energy to the atmosphere around it, so does a heated body give out part of its heat energy to the ethereal medium around it. When, however, we consider the rates of motion of these energies through their respective media, there is a mighty difference between the two, sound travelling through the air with the velocity of 1100 feet a second, while radiant energy moves over no less a space than 188,000 miles in the same portion of time.

Chemical Separation.

169. We now come to the energy denoted by chemical separation, such as we possess when we have coal or carbon in one place, and oxygen in another. Very evi-

dently this form of energy of position is transmuted into *heat* when we burn the coal, or cause it to combine with the oxygen of the air; and generally, whenever chemical combination takes place, we have the production of heat, even although other circumstances may interfere to prevent its recognition.

Now, in accordance with the principle of conservation, it may be expected that, if a definite quantity of carbon or of hydrogen be burned under given circumstances, there will be a definite production of heat; that is to say, a ton of coals or of coke, when burned, will give us so many heat units, and neither more or less. We may, no doubt, burn our ton in such a way as to economize more or less of the heat produced; but, as far as the mere production of heat is concerned, if the quantity and quality of the material burned and the circumstances of combustion be the same, we expect the same amount of heat.

164. The following table, derived from the researches of Andrews, and those of Favre and Silbermann, shows us how many units of heat we may get by burning a kilogramme of various substances.

Units *of* Heat *developed by* Combustion *in* Oxygen.

Substance Burned.	Kilogrammes of Water raised 1° C. by the combustion of one kilogramme of each substance.
Hydrogen	34,135
Carbon	7,990
Sulphur	2,263

Substance Burned.	Kilogrammes of Water raised 1° C. by the combustion of one kilogramme of each substance.
Phosphorus	5,747
Zinc	1,301
Iron	1,576
Tin	1,233
Olefiant Gas	11,000
Alcohol	7,016

165. There are other methods, besides combustion, by which chemical combination takes place.

When, for instance, we plunge a piece of metallic iron into a solution of copper, we find that when we take it out, its surface is covered with copper. Part of the iron has been dissolved, taking the place of the copper, which has therefore been thrown, in its metallic state, upon the surface of the iron. Now, in this operation heat is given out—we have in fact burned, or oxidized, the iron, and we are thus furnished with a means of arranging the metals, beginning with that which gives out most heat, when used to displace the metal at the other extremity of the series.

166. The following list has been formed, on this principle, by Dr. Andrews:—

1. Zinc
2. Iron
3. Lead
4. Copper
5. Mercury
6. Silver
7. Platinum

—that is to say, the metal platinum can be displaced by any other metal of the series, but we shall get most heat if we use zinc to displace it.

We may therefore assume that if we displace a definite quantity of platinum by a definite quantity of zinc, we shall get a definite amount of heat. Suppose, however, that instead of performing the operation in one step, we make two of it. Let us, for instance, first of all displace copper by means of zinc, and then platinum by means of copper. Is it not possible that the one of these processes may be more fruitful in heat giving than the other? Now, Andrews has shown us that we cannot gain an advantage over Nature in this way, and that if we use our zinc first of all to displace iron, or copper, or lead, and then use this metal to displace platinum, we shall obtain just the very same amount of heat as if we had used the zinc to displace the platinum at once.

167. It ought here to be mentioned that, very generally, chemical action is accompanied with a change of molecular condition.

A solid, for instance, may be changed into a liquid, or a gas into a liquid. Sometimes the one change counteracts the other as far as apparent heat is concerned; but sometimes, too, they co-operate together to increase the result. Thus, when a gas is absorbed by water, much heat is evolved, and we may suppose the result to be due in part to chemical combination, and in part to the condensation of the gas into a liquid, by which means its latent heat is rendered sensible. On the other hand, when a liquid unites with a solid, or when two solids unite with one another, and the product is a liquid, we have very often the absorption of heat, the heat rendered latent by the dissolution of the solid being more than that generated by combination. Freezing mixtures owe their cooling properties to this cause; thus, if snow and salt be mixed together, they liquefy each other, and the result is brine of a temperature much lower than that of either the ingredients.

168. When heterogeneous metals, such as zinc and copper, are soldered together, we have apparently a conversion of the energy of chemical separation into that of *electrical separation*. This was first suggested by Volta as the origin of the electrical separation which we see in the voltaic current, and recently its existence has been distinctly proved by Sir W. Thomson.

To render manifest this conversion of energy, let us solder a piece of zinc and copper together—if we now test the bar by means of a delicate electrometer we shall find that the zinc is positively, while the copper is negatively, electrified. We have here, therefore, an instance of the transmutation of one form of energy of position into another; so much energy of chemical separation disappearing in order to produce so much electrical separation. This explains the fact recorded in Art. 93, where we saw that if a battery be insulated and its poles kept apart, the one will be charged with positive, and the other with negative, electricity.

169. But further, when such a voltaic battery is in action, we have a transmutation of chemical separation into *electricity in motion*. To see this, let us consider what takes place in such a battery.

Here no doubt the sources of electrical excitement are the points of contact of the zinc and platinum, where, as we see by our last article, we have electrical separation produced. But this of itself would not produce a current, for an electrical current implies very considerable energy, and must be fed by something. Now, in the voltaic battery we have two things which accompany each other, and which are manifestly connected together. In the first place we have the combustion, or at least the oxidation and dissolution, of the zinc; and we have, secondly, the production of a powerful current. Now, evidently, the first of these is that which feeds the second, or, in other words, the energy of chemical separation of the metallic zinc is transmuted into that of an electrical current, the zinc being virtually burned in the process of transmutation.

170. Finally, as far as we are aware, the energy of chemical separation is not directly transmuted into radiant light and heat.

Electrical Separation.

171. In the first place the energy of electrical separation is obviously transmuted into that of *visible motion*, when two oppositely electrified bodies approach each other.

172. Again, it is transmuted into a *current of electricity*, and ultimately into heat, when a spark passes between two oppositely electrified bodies.

It ought, therefore, to be borne in mind that when the flash is seen there is no longer electricity, what we see being merely air, or some other material, intensely heated by the discharge. Thus a man might be rendered insensible by a flash of lightning without his seeing the flash—for the effect of the discharge upon the man, and its effect in heating the air, might be phenomena so nearly simultaneous that the man might become insensible before he could perceive the flash.

Electricity in Motion.

173. This energy is transmuted into that of *visible motion* when two wires conveying electrical currents in the same direction attract each other. When, for instance, two circular currents float on water, both going in the direction of the hands of a watch, we have seen from Art. 100 that they will move towards each other. Now, here there is, in truth, a lessening of the intensity of each current when the motion is taking place, for

we know (Art. 104) that when a circuit is moved into the presence of another circuit conveying a current, there is produced by induction a current in the opposite direction; and hence we perceive that, when two similar currents approach each other, each is diminished by means of this inductive influence—in fact, a certain amount of current energy disappears from existence in order that an equivalent amount of the energy of visible motion may be produced.

174. Electricity in motion is transmuted into *heat* during the passage of a current along a thin wire, or any badly conducting substance—the wire is heated in consequence, and may even become white hot. Most frequently the energy of an electric current is spent in heating the wires and other materials that form the circuit. Now, the energy of such a current is fed by the burning or oxidation of the metal (generally zinc) which is used in the circuit, so that the ultimate effect of this combustion is the heating of the various wires and other materials through which the current passes.

175. We may, in truth, burn or oxidize zinc in two ways—we may oxidize it, as we have just seen, in the voltaic battery, and we shall find that by the combustion of a kilogramme of zinc a definite amount of heat is produced. Or we may oxidize our zinc by dissolving it in acid in a single vessel, when, without going through the intermediate process of a current, we shall get just as much heat out of a kilogramme of zinc as we did in the

former case. In fact, whether we oxidize our zinc by the battery, or in the ordinary way, the quantity of heat produced will always bear the same relation to the quantity of zinc consumed; the only difference being that, in the ordinary way of oxidizing zinc, the heat is generated in the vessel containing the zinc and acid, while in the battery it may make its appearance a thousand miles away, if we have a sufficiently long wire to convey our current.

176. This is, perhaps, the right place for alluding to a discovery of Peltier, that a current of positive electricity passing across a junction of bismuth and antimony in the direction from the bismuth to the antimony appears to produce cold.

To understand the significance of this fact we must consider it in connection with the thermo-electric current, which we have seen, from Art. 161, is established in a circuit of bismuth and antimony, of which one junction is hotter than the other. Suppose we have a

Fig. 14.

circuit of this kind with both its junctions at the temperature of 100° C. to begin with. Suppose, next, that while we protect one junction, we expose the other to the open air—it will, of course, lose heat, so that the protected junction will now be hotter than the other. The consequence will be (Art. 161) that a current of positive electricity will pass along the protected junction from the bismuth to the antimony.

Now, here we have an apparent anomaly, for the circuit is cooling—that is to say, it is losing energy—but at the very same time it is manifesting energy in another shape, namely, in that of an electric current, which is circulating round it. Clearly, then, some of the heat of this circuit must be spent in generating this current; in fact, we should expect the circuit to act as a heat engine, only producing current energy instead of mechanical energy, and hence (Art. 152) we should expect to see a conveyance of heat from the hotter to the colder parts of the circuit. Now, this is precisely what the current does, for, passing along the hotter junction, in the direction of the arrow-head, it cools that junction, and heats the colder one at c,—in other words, it carries heat from the hotter to the colder parts of the circuit. We should have been very much surprised had such a current cooled c and heated н, for then we should have had a manifestation of current energy, accompanied with the conveyance of heat from a colder to a hotter substance, which is against the principle of Art. 152.

177. Finally, the energy of electricity in motion is converted into that of *chemical separation*, when a current of electricity is made to decompose a body. Part of the energy of the current is spent in this process, and we shall get so much less heat from it in consequence. Suppose, for instance, that by oxidizing so much zinc in the battery we get, under ordinary circum-

stances, 100 units of heat. Let us, however, set the battery to decompose water, and we shall probably find that by oxidizing the same amount of zinc we get now only 80 units of heat. Clearly, then, the deficiency or 20 units have gone to decompose the water. Now, if we explode the mixed gases which are the result of the decomposition, we shall get back these 20 units of heat precisely, and neither more nor less; and thus we see that amid all such changes the quantity of energy remains the same.

Radiant Energy.

178. This form of energy is converted into *absorbed heat* whenever it falls upon an opaque substance—some of it, however, is generally conveyed away by reflexion, but the remainder is absorbed by the body, and consequently heats it.

It is a curious question to ask what becomes of the radiant light from the sun that is not absorbed either by the planets of our system, or by any of the stars. We can only reply to such a question, that *as far as we can judge from our present knowledge*, the radiant energy that is not absorbed must be conceived to be traversing space at the rate of 188,000 miles a second.

179. There is only one more transmutation of radiant energy that we know of, and that is when it promotes *chemical separation.* Thus, certain rays of the sun are known to have the power of decomposing chloride of

silver, and other chemical compounds. Now, in all such cases there is a transmutation of radiant energy into that of chemical separation. The sun's rays, too, decompose carbonic acid in the leaves of plants, the carbon going to form the woody fibre of the plant, while the oxygen is set free into the air; and of course a certain proportion of the energy of the solar rays is consumed in promoting this change, and we have so much less heating effect in consequence.

But all the solar rays have not this power—for the property of promoting chemical change is confined to the blue and violet rays, and some others which are not visible to the eye. Now, these rays are entirely absent from the radiation of bodies at a comparatively low temperature, such as an ordinary red heat, so that a photographer would find it impossible to obtain the picture of a red-hot body, whose only light was in itself.

180. The actinic, or chemically active, rays of the sun decompose carbonic acid in the leaves of plants, and they disappear in consequence, or are absorbed; this may, therefore, be the reason why very few such rays are either reflected or transmitted from a sun-lit leaf, in consequence of which the photographer finds it difficult to obtain an image of such a leaf; in other words, the rays which would have produced a chemical change on his photographic plate have all been used up by the leaf for peculiar purposes of its own.

181. And here it is important to bear in mind that

while animals in the act of breathing consume the oxygen of the air, turning it into carbonic acid, plants, on the other hand, restore the oxygen to the air; thus the two kingdoms, the animal and the vegetable, work into each other's hands, and the purity of the atmosphere is kept up.

CHAPTER V.

HISTORICAL SKETCH: THE DISSIPATION OF ENERGY.

182. In the last chapter we have endeavoured to exhibit the various transmutations of energy, and, while doing so, to bring forward evidence in favour of the theory of conservation, showing that it enables us to couple together known laws, and also to discover new ones—showing, in fine, that it bears about with it all the marks of a true hypothesis.

It may now, perhaps, be instructive to look back and endeavour to trace the progress of this great conception, from its first beginning among the ancients, up to its triumphant establishment by the labours of Joule and his fellow-workers.

183. Mathematicians inform us that if matter consists of atoms or small parts, which are actuated by forces depending only upon the distances between these parts, and not upon the velocity, then it may be demonstrated that the law of conservation of energy will hold good. Thus we see that conceptions regarding atoms and their

forces are allied to conceptions regarding energy. A medium of some sort pervading space seems also necessary to our theory. In fine, a universe composed of atoms, with some sort of medium between them, is to be regarded as the machine, and the laws of energy as the laws of working of this machine. It may be that a theory of atoms of this sort, with a medium between them, is not after all the simplest, but we are probably not yet prepared for any more general hypothesis. Now, we have only to look to our own solar system, in order to see on a large scale an illustration of this conception, for there we have the various heavenly bodies attracting one another, with forces depending only on the distances between them, and independent of the velocities; and we have likewise a medium of some sort, in virtue of which radiant energy is conveyed from the sun to the earth. Perhaps we shall not greatly err if we regard a molecule as representing on a small scale something analogous to the solar system, while the various atoms which constitute the molecule may be likened to the various bodies of the solar system. The short historical sketch which we are about to give will embrace, therefore, along with energy, the progress of thought and speculation with respect to atoms and also with respect to a medium, inasmuch as these subjects are intimately connected with the doctrines of energy.

Heraclitus on Energy.

184. Heraclitus, who flourished at Ephesus, B.C. 500, declared that fire was the great cause, and that all things were in a perpetual flux. Such an expression will no doubt be regarded as very vague in these days of precise physical statements; and yet it seems clear that Heraclitus must have had a vivid conception of the innate restlessness and energy of the universe, a conception allied in character to, and only less precise than that of modern philosophers, who regard matter as essentially dynamical.

Democritus on Atoms.

185. Democritus, who was born 470 B.C., was the originator of the doctrine of atoms, a doctrine which in the hands of John Dalton has enabled the human mind to lay hold of the laws which regulate chemical changes, as well as to picture to itself what is there taking place. Perhaps there is no doctrine that has nowadays a more intimate connection with the industries of life than this of atoms, and it is probable that no intelligent director of chemical industry among civilized nations fails to picture to his own mind, by means of this doctrine, the inner nature of the changes which he sees with his eyes. Now, it is a curious circumstance that Bacon should have lighted upon this very doctrine of atoms, in order to point one of his philosophical morals.

"Nor is it less an evil" (says he), "that in their philosophies and contemplations men spend their labour in investigating and treating of the first principles of things, and the extreme limits of nature, when all that is useful and of avail in operation is to be found in what is intermediate. Hence it happens that men continue to abstract Nature till they arrive at potential and unformed matter; and again they continue to divide Nature, until they have arrived at the atom; things which, even if true, can be of little use in helping on the fortunes of men."

Surely we ought to learn a lesson from these remarks of the great Father of experimental science, and be very cautious before we dismiss any branch of knowledge or train of thought as essentially unprofitable.

Aristotle on a Medium.

186. As regards the existence of a medium, it is remarked by Whewell that the ancients also caught a glimpse of the idea of a medium, by which the qualities of bodies, as colours and sounds are perceived, and he quotes the following from Aristotle :—

"In a void there could be no difference of up and down; for, as in nothing there are no differences, so there are none in a privation or negation."

Upon this the historian of science remarks, "It is easily seen that such a mode of reasoning elevates the familiar forms of language, and the intellectual connexions of terms, to a supremacy over facts."

Nevertheless, may it not be replied that our conceptions

of matter are deduced from the familiar experience, that certain portions of space affect us in a certain manner; and, consequently, are we not entitled to say there must be something where we experience the difference of up or down? Is there, after all, a very great difference between this argument and that of modern physicists in favour of a plenum, who tell us that matter cannot act where it is not?

Aristotle seems also to have entertained the idea that light is not any body, or the emanation of any body (for that, he says, would be a kind of body), and that therefore light is an energy or act.

The Ideas of the Ancients were not Prolific

187. These quotations render it evident that the ancients had, in some way, grasped the idea of the essential unrest and energy of things. They had also the idea of small particles or atoms, and, finally, of a medium of some sort. And yet these ideas were not prolific—they gave rise to nothing new.

Now, while the historian of science is unquestionably right in his criticism of the ancients, that their ideas were not distinct and appropriate to the facts, yet we have seen that they were not wholly ignorant of the most profound and deeply-seated principles of the material universe. In the great hymn chanted by Nature, the fundamental notes were early heard, but yet it required long centuries of patient waiting for the practised ear of the skilled musician to appreciate the mighty harmony aright. Or, perhaps, the attempts of the ancients were as the sketches of a child who just contrives to exhibit, in a rude way, the leading outlines of a building; while the conceptions of the practised physicist are more allied to those of the architect, or, at least, of one who has realized, to some extent, the architect's views.

188. The ancients possessed great genius and intellectual power, but they were deficient in physical conceptions, and, in consequence, their ideas were not prolific. It cannot indeed be said that we of the present age are deficient in such conceptions; nevertheless, it may be questioned whether there is not a tendency to rush into the opposite extreme, and to work physical conceptions to an excess. Let us be cautious that in avoiding Scylla, we do not rush into Charybdis. For the universe has more than one point of view, and there are possibly regions which will not yield their treasures to the most determined physicists, armed only with kilogrammes and metres and standard clocks.

Descartes, Newton, and Huyghens on a Medium.

189. In modern times Descartes, author of the vertical hypothesis, necessarily presupposed the existence of a medium in inter-planetary spaces, but on the other hand he was one of the originators of that idea which regards light as a series of particles shot out from a luminous body. Newton likewise conceived the existence of a

medium, although he became an advocate of the theory of emission. It is to Huyghens that the credit belongs of having first conceived the undulatory theory of light with sufficient distinctness to account for double refraction. After him, Young, Fresnel, and their followers, have greatly developed the theory, enabling it to account for the most complicated and wonderful phenomena.

Bacon on Heat.

190. With regard to the nature of heat, Bacon, whatever may be thought of his arguments, seems clearly to have recognized it as a species of motion. He says, "From these instances, viewed together and individually, the nature of which heat is the limitation seems to be motion;" and again he says, "But when we say of motion that it stands in the place of a genus to heat, we mean to convey, not that *heat* generates *motion* or *motion heat* (although even both may be true in some cases), but that essential heat is motion and nothing else."

Nevertheless it required nearly three centuries before the true theory of heat was sufficiently rooted to develop into a productive hypothesis.

Principle of Virtual Velocities.

191. In a previous chapter we have already detailed the labours in respect of heat of Davy, Rumford, and Joule. Galileo and Newton, if they did not grasp the dynamical nature of heat, had yet a clear conception of

machine—how to say to it, At what rate can you labour? how much work can you turn out in a day? It is necessary, in fact, to have the clearest possible idea of what work is.

Our readers will see from all this that men are not likely to err in their method of measuring work. The principles of measurement have been stamped as it were with a brand into the very heart and brain of humanity. To the employer of machinery or of human labour, a false method of measuring work simply means ruin; he is likely, therefore, to take the greatest possible pains to arrive at accuracy in his determination.

Perpetual Motion.

193. Now, amid the crowd of workers smarting from the curse of labour, there rises up every now and then an enthusiast, who seeks to escape by means of an artifice from this insupportable tyranny of work. Why not construct a machine that will go on giving you work without limit without the necessity of being fed in any way. Nature must have some weak point in her armour; there must surely be some way of getting round her; she is only tyrannous on the surface, and in order to stimulate our ingenuity, but will yield with pleasure to the persistence of genius.

Now, what can the man of science say to such an enthusiast? He cannot tell him that he is intimately acquainted with all the forces of Nature, and can prove that perpetual motion is impossible; for, in truth, he knows very little of these forces. But he does think that he has entered into the spirit and design of Nature, and therefore he denies at once the possibility of such a machine. But he denies it intelligently, and works out this denial of his into a theory which enables him to discover numerous and valuable relations between the properties of matter—produces, in fact, the laws of energy and the great principle of conservation.

Theory of Conservation.

194. We have thus endeavoured to give a short sketch of the history of energy, including its allied problems, up to the dawn of the strictly scientific period. We have seen that the unfruitfulness of the earlier views was due to a want of scientific clearness in the conceptions entertained, and we have now to say a few words regarding the theory of conservation.

Here also the way was pointed out by two philosophers, namely, Grove in this country, and Mayer on the continent, who showed certain relations between the various forms of energy; the name of Séguin ought likewise to be mentioned. Nevertheless, to Joule belongs the honour of establishing the theory on an incontrovertible basis: for, indeed, this is pre-eminently a case where speculation has to be tested by unimpeachable experimental evidence. Here the magnitude of the principle is so vast, and its importance is so great, that it requires the strong fire of genius, joined to the patient labours of the scientific experimentalist, to forge the rough ore into a good weapon that will cleave its way through all obstacles into the very citadel of Nature, and into her most secret recesses.

Following closely upon the labours of Joule, we have those of William and James Thomson, Helmholtz, Rankine, Clausius, Tait, Andrews, Maxwell, who, along with many others, have advanced the subject; and while Joule gave his chief attention to the laws which regulate the transmutation of mechanical energy into heat, Thomson, Rankine, and Clausius gave theirs to the converse problem, or that which relates to the transmutation of heat into mechanical energy. Thomson, especially, has pushed forward so resolutely from this point of view that he has succeeded in grasping a principle scarcely inferior in importance to that of the conservation of energy itself, and of this principle it behoves us now to speak.

Dissipation of Energy.

195. Joule, we have said, proved the law according to which work may be changed into heat; and Thomson and others, that according to which heat may be changed into work. Now, it occurred to Thomson that there was a very important and significant difference between these two laws, consisting in the fact that, while you can with the greatest ease transform work into heat, you can by no method in your power transform all the heat back

again into work. In fact, the process is not a reversible one; and the consequence is that the mechanical energy of the universe is becoming every day more and more changed into heat.

It is easily seen that if the process were reversible, one form of a perpetual motion would not be impossible. For, without attempting to create energy by a machine, all that would be needed for a perpetual motion would be the means of utilizing the vast stores of heat that lie in all the substances around us, and converting them into work. The work would no doubt, by means of friction and otherwise, be ultimately reconverted into heat; but if the process be reversible, the heat could again be converted into work, and so on for ever. But the irreversibility of the process puts a stop to all this. In fact, I may convince myself by rubbing a metal button on a piece of wood how easily work can be converted into heat, while the mind completely fails to suggest any method by which this heat can be reconverted into work.

Now, if this process goes on, and always in one direction, there can be no doubt about the issue. The mechanical energy of the universe will be more and more transformed into universally diffused heat, until the universe will no longer be a fit abode for living beings.

The conclusion is a startling one, and, in order to bring it more vividly before our readers, let us now proceed to acquaint ourselves with the various forms of useful energy that are at present at our disposal, and at the same time endeavour to trace the ultimate sources of these supplies.

Natural Energies and their Sources.

196. Of energy in repose we have the following varieties:—(1.) The energy of fuel. (2.) That of food. (3.) That of a head of water. (4.) That which may be derived from the tides. (5.) The energy of chemical separation implied in native sulphur, native iron, &c.

Then, with regard to energy in action, we have mainly the following varieties:—

(1.) The energy of air in motion. (2.) That of water in motion.

Fuel.

197. Let us begin first with the energy implied in fuel. We can, of course, burn fuel, or cause it to combine with the oxygen of the air; and we are thereby provided with large quantities of heat of high temperature, by means of which we may not only warm ourselves and cook our food, but also drive our heat-engines, using it, in fact, as a source of mechanical power.

Fuel is of two varieties—wood and coal. Now, if we consider the origin of these we shall see that they are produced by the sun's rays. Certain of these rays, as we have already remarked (Art. 180), decompose carbonic acid in the leaves of plants, setting free the oxygen, while the carbon is used for the structure or wood of the plant. Now, the energy of these rays is spent in this process, and, indeed, there is not enough of such energy left to produce a good photographic impression of the leaf of a plant, because it is all spent in making wood.

We thus see that the energy implied in wood is derived from the sun's rays, and the same remark applies to coal. Indeed, the only difference between wood and coal is one of age: wood being recently turned out from Nature's laboratory, while thousands of years have elapsed since coal formed the leaves of living plants.

198. We are, therefore, perfectly justified in saying that the energy of fuel is derived from the sun's rays;* coal being the store which Nature has laid up as a species of capital for us, while wood is our precarious yearly income.

We are thus at present very much in the position of a young heir, who has only recently come into his estate, and who, not content with the income, is rapidly squandering his realized property. This subject has been forcibly brought before us by Professor Jevons, who has remarked that not only are we spending our capital, but we are spending the most available and valuable part of it. For we are now using the surface coal; but a time will come when this will be exhausted, and we shall be compelled to go deep down for our

* This fact seems to have been known at a comparatively early period to Herschel and the elder Stephenson.

supplies. Now, regarded as a source of energy, such supplies, if far down, will be less effective, for we have to deduct the amount of energy requisite in order to bring them to the surface. The result is that we must contemplate a time, however far distant, when our supplies of coal will be exhausted, and we shall be compelled to resort to other sources of energy.

Food.

199. The energy of food is analogous to that of fuel, and serves similar purposes. For just as fuel may be used either for producing heat or for doing work, so food has a twofold office to perform. In the first place, by its gradual oxidation, it keeps up the temperature of the body; and in the next place it is used as a source of energy, on which to draw for the performance of work. Thus a man or a horse that works a great deal requires to eat more food than if he does not work at all. Thus, also, a prisoner condemned to hard labour requires a better diet than one who does not work, and a soldier during the fatigues of war finds it necessary to eat more than during a time of peace.

Our food may be either of animal or vegetable origin— if it be the latter, it is immediately derived, like fuel, from the energy of the sun's rays; but if it be the former, the only difference is that it has passed through the body of an animal before coming to us: the animal has eaten grass, and we have eaten the animal.

In fact, we make use of the animal not only as a variety of nutritious food, but also to enable us indirectly to utilize those vegetable products, such as grasses, which we could not make use of directly with our present digestive organs.

Head of Water.

200. The energy of a head of water, like that of fuel and food, is brought about by the sun's rays. For the sun vaporizes the water, which, condensed again in upland districts, becomes available as a head of water.

There is, however, the difference that fuel and food are due to the actinic power of the sun's rays, while the evaporation and condensation of water are caused rather by their heating effect.

Tidal Energy.

201. The energy derived from the tides has, however, a different origin. In Art. 133 we have endeavoured to show how the moon acts upon the fluid portions of our globe, the result of this action being a very gradual stoppage of the energy of rotation of the earth.

It is, therefore, to this motion of rotation that we must look as the origin of any available energy derived from tidal mills.

Native Sulphur, &c.

202. The last variety of available energy of position in our list is that implied in native sulphur, native iron, &c. It has been remarked by Professor Tait, to whom this method of reviewing our forces is due, that this may be the primeval form of energy, and that the interior of the earth may, as far as we know, be wholly composed of matter in its uncombined form. As a source of available energy it is, however, of no practical importance.

Air and Water in Motion.

203. We proceed next to those varieties of available energy which represent motion, the chief of which are air in motion and water in motion. It is owing to the former that the mariner spreads his sail, and carries his vessel from one part of the earth's surface to another, and it is likewise owing to the same influence that the windmill grinds our corn. Again, water in motion is used perhaps even more frequently than air in motion as a source of motive power.

Both these varieties of energy are due without doubt to the heating effect of the sun's rays. We may, therefore, affirm that with the exception of the totally insignificant supply of native sulphur, &c., and the small number of tidal mills which may be in operation, all our available energy is due to the sun.

The Sun—a Source of High Temperature Heat.

204. Let us, therefore, now for a moment direct our attention to that most wonderful source of energy, the Sun.

We have here a vast reservoir of high temperature heat; now, this is a kind of superior energy which has always been in much request. Numberless attempts have been made to construct a perpetual light, just as similar attempts have been made to construct a perpetual motion, with this difference, that a perpetual light was supposed to result from magical powers, while a perpetual motion was attributed to mechanical skill.

Sir Walter Scott alludes to this belief in his description of the grave of Michael Scott, which is made to contain a perpetual light. Thus the Monk who buried the wizard tells William of Deloraine—

> "Lo, Warrior! now the Cross of Red
> Points to the Grave of the mighty dead;
> Within it burns a wondrous light,
> To chase the spirits that love the night.
> That lamp shall burn unquenchably
> Until the eternal doom shall be."

And again, when the tomb was opened, we read—

> "I would you had been there to see
> How the light broke forth so gloriously,
> Stream'd upward to the chancel roof,
> And through the galleries far aloof!
> No earthly flame blazed e'er so bright."

No earthly flame—there the poet was right—certainly not of this earth, where light and all other forms of superior energy are essentially evanescent.

A Perpetual Light Impossible.

205. In truth, our readers will at once perceive that a perpetual light is only another name for a perpetual motion, because we can always derive visible energy out of high temperature heat—indeed, we do so every day in our steam engines.

When, therefore, we burn coal, and cause it to combine with the oxygen of the air, we derive from the process a large amount of high temperature heat. But is it not possible, our readers may ask, to take the carbonic acid which results from the combustion, and by means of low temperature heat, of which we have always abundance at our disposal, change it back again into carbon and oxygen? All this would be possible if what may be termed the temperature of disassociation—that is to say, the temperature at which carbonic acid separates into its constituents—were a low temperature, and it would also be possible if rays from a source of low temperature possessed sufficient actinic power to decompose carbonic acid.

But neither of these is the case. Nature will not be caught in a trap of this kind. As if for the very purpose of stopping all such speculations, the temperatures of disassociation for such substances as carbonic acid are very high, and the actinic rays capable of causing their decomposition belong only to sources of exceedingly high temperature, such as the sun.*

Is the Sun an Exception?

206. We may, therefore, take it for granted that a perpetual light, like a perpetual motion, is an impossibility; and we have then to inquire if the same argument applies to our sun, or if an exception is to be made in his favour. Does the sun stand upon a footing of his own, or is it merely a question of time with him, as with all other instances of high temperature heat? Before attempting to answer this question let us inquire into the probable origin of the sun's heat.

Origin of the Sun's Heat.

207. Now, some might be disposed to cut the Gordian knot of such an inquiry by asserting that our luminary was at first created hot; yet the scientific mind finds itself disinclined to repose upon such an assertion. We pick up a round pebble from the beach, and at once acknowledge there has been some physical cause for the shape into which it has been worn. And so with regard to the heat of the sun, we must ask ourselves if there be not some cause not wholly imaginary, but one which we know, or at least suspect, to be perhaps still in operation, which can account for the heat of the sun.

Now, here it is more easy to show what cannot

---

* This remark is due to Sir William Thomson.

account for the sun's heat than what can do so. We may, for instance, be perfectly certain that it cannot have been caused by chemical action. The most probable theory is that which was first worked out by Helmholtz and Thomson;* and which attributes the heat of the sun to the primeval energy of position possessed by its particles. In other words, it is supposed that these particles originally existed at a great distance from each other, and that, being endowed with the force of gravitation, they have since gradually come together, while in this process heat has been generated just as it would be if a stone were dropped from the top of a cliff towards the earth.

208. Nor is this case wholly imaginary, but we have some reason for thinking that it may still be in operation in the case of certain nebulæ which, both in their constitution as revealed by the spectroscope, and in their general appearance, impress the beholder with the idea that they are not yet fully condensed into their ultimate shape and size.

If we allow that by this means our luminary has obtained his wonderful store of high-class energy, we have yet to inquire to what extent this operation is going on at the present moment. Is it only a thing of the past, or is it a thing also of the present? I think we may reply that the sun cannot be condensing very fast, at least, within historical times. For if the

---

* Mayer and Waterston seem first to have caught the rudiments of this idea.

sun were sensibly larger than at present his total eclipse by the moon would be impossible. Now, such eclipses have taken place, at any rate, for several thousands of years. Doubtless a small army of meteors may be falling into our luminary, which would by this fall tend to augment his heat; yet the supply derived from this source must surely be insignificant. But if the sun be not at present condensing so fast as to derive any sufficient heat from this process, and if his energy be very sparingly recruited from without, it necessarily follows that he is in the position of a man whose expenditure exceeds his income. He is living upon his capital, and is destined to share the fate of all who act in a similar manner. We must, therefore, contemplate a future period when he will be poorer in energy than he is at present, and a period still further in the future when he will altogether cease to shine.

Probable Fate of the Universe.

209. If this be the fate of the high temperature energy of the universe, let us think for a moment what will happen to its visible energy. We have spoken already about a medium pervading space, the office of which appears to be to degrade and ultimately extinguish all differential motion, just as it tends to reduce and ultimately equalize all difference of temperature. Thus the universe would ultimately become an equally heated mass, utterly worthless as far as the production of work is concerned, since such production depends upon difference of temperature.

Although, therefore, in a strictly mechanical sense, there is a conservation of energy, yet, as regards usefulness or fitness for living beings, the energy of the universe is in process of deterioration. Universally diffused heat forms what we may call the great wasteheap of the universe, and this is growing larger year by year. At present it does not sensibly obtrude itself, but who knows that the time may not arrive when we shall be practically conscious of its growing bigness?

210. It will be seen that in this chapter we have regarded the universe, not as a collection of matter, but rather as an energetic agent—in fact, as a lamp. Now, it has been well pointed out by Thomson, that looked at in this light, the universe is a system that had a beginning and must have an end; for a process of degradation cannot be eternal. If we could view the universe as a candle not lit, then it is perhaps conceivable to regard it as having been always in existence; but if we regard it rather as a candle that has been lit, we become absolutely certain that it cannot have been burning from eternity, and that a time will come when it will cease to burn. We are led to look to a beginning in which the particles of matter were in a diffuse chaotic state, but endowed with the power of gravitation, and we are led to look to an end in which the whole universe will be one equally heated inert mass, and from which everything like life or motion or beauty will have utterly gone away.

CHAPTER VI.

THE POSITION OF LIFE.

211. WE have hitherto confined ourselves almost entirely to a discussion of the laws of energy, as these affect inanimate matter, and have taken little or no account of the position of life. We have been content very much to remain spectators of the contest, apparently forgetful that we are at all concerned in the issue. But the conflict is not one which admits of on-lookers,—it is a universal conflict in which we must all take our share. It may not, therefore, be amiss if we endeavour to ascertain, as well as we can, our true position.

Twofold nature of Equilibrium.

212. One of our earliest mechanical lessons is on the twofold nature of equilibrium. We are told that this may be of two kinds, *stable* and *unstable*, and a very good illustration of these two kinds is furnished by an egg. Let us take a smooth level table, and place an egg upon it; we all know in what manner the egg will lie

on the table. It will remain at rest, that is to say, it will be in equilibrium; and not only so, but it will be in stable equilibrium. To prove this, let us try to displace it with our finger, and we shall find that when we remove the pressure the egg will speedily return to its previous position, and will come to rest after one or two oscillations. Furthermore, it has required a sensible expenditure of energy to displace the egg. All this we express by saying that the egg is in stable equilibrium.

Mechanical Instability.

213. And now let us try to balance the egg upon its longer axis. Probably, a sufficient amount of care will enable us to achieve this also. But the operation is a difficult one, and requires great delicacy of touch, and even after we have succeeded we do not know how long our success may last. The slightest impulse from without, the merest breath of air, may be sufficient to overturn the egg, which is now most evidently in unstable equilibrium. If the egg be thus balanced at the very edge of the table, it is quite probable that in a few minutes it may topple over upon the floor; it is what we may call *an even chance* whether it will do so, or merely fall upon the table. Not that mere chance has anything to do with it, or that its movements are without a cause, but we mean that its movements are decided by some external impulse so exceedingly small as to be utterly beyond our powers of observation. In fact, before making the trial

we have carefully removed everything like a current of air, or want of level, or external impulse of any kind, so that when the egg falls we are completely unable to assign the origin of the impulse that has caused it to do so.

214. Now, if the egg happens to fall over the table upon the floor, there is a somewhat considerable transmutation of energy; for the energy of position of the egg, due to the height which it occupied on the table, has all at once been changed into energy of motion, in the first place, and into heat in the second, when the egg comes into contact with the floor.

If, however, the egg happens to fall upon the table, the transmutation of energy is comparatively small.

It thus appears that it depends upon some external impulse, so infinitesimally small as to elude our observation, whether the egg shall fall upon the floor and give rise to a comparatively large transmutation of energy, or whether it shall fall upon the table and give rise to a transmutation comparatively small.

Chemical Instability.

215. We thus see that a body, or system, in unstable equilibrium may become subject to a very considerable transmutation of energy, arising out of a very small cause, or antecedent. In the case now mentioned, the force is that of gravitation, the arrangement being one of visible mechanical instability. But we may have a sub-

stance, or system, in which the force at work is not gravity, but chemical affinity, and the substance, or system, may, under certain peculiar conditions, become *chemically unstable*.

When a substance is chemically unstable, it means that the slightest impulse of any kind may determine a chemical change, just as in the case of the egg the slightest impulse from without occasioned a mechanical displacement.

In fine, a substance, or system, chemically unstable bears a relation to chemical affinity somewhat similar to that which a mechanically unstable system bears to gravity. Gunpowder is a familiar instance of a chemically unstable substance. Here the slightest spark may prove the precursor of a sudden chemical change, accompanied by the instantaneous and violent generation of a vast volume of heated gas. The various explosive compounds, such as gun-cotton, nitro-glycerine, the fulminates, and many more, are all instances of structures which are chemically unstable.

Machines are of two kinds.

216. When we speak of a structure, or a machine, or a system, we simply mean a number of individual particles associated together in producing some definite result. Thus, the solar system, a timepiece, a rifle, are examples of inanimate machines; while an animal, a human being, an army, are examples of animated struc-

tures or machines. Now, such machines or structures are of two kinds, which differ from one another not only in the object sought, but also in the means of attaining that object.

217. In the first place, we have structures or machines in which systematic action is the object aimed at, and in which all the arrangements are of a conservative nature, the element of instability being avoided as much as possible. The solar system, a timepiece, a steam-engine at work, are examples of such machines, and the characteristic of all such is their *calculability*. Thus the skilled astronomer can tell, with the utmost precision, in what place the moon or the planet Venus will be found this time next year. Or again, the excellence of a timepiece consists in its various hands pointing accurately in a certain direction after a certain interval of time. In like manner we may safely count upon a steamship making so many knots an hour, at least while the outward conditions remain the same. In all these cases we make our calculations, and we are not deceived—the end sought is regularity of action, and the means employed is a stable arrangement of the forces of nature.

218. Now, the characteristics of the other class of machines are precisely the reverse.

Here the object aimed at is not a regular, but a sudden and violent transmutation of energy, while the means employed are unstable arrangements of natural forces.

A rifle at full cock, with a delicate hair-trigger, is a very good instance of such a machine, where the slightest touch from without may bring about the explosion of the gunpowder, and the propulsion of the ball with a very great velocity. Now, such machines are eminently characterized by their *incalculability*.

219. To make our meaning clear, let us suppose that two sportsmen go out hunting together, each with a good rifle and a good pocket chronometer. After a hard day's work, the one turns to his companion and says:—" It is now six o'clock by my watch; we had better rest ourselves," upon which the other looks at his watch, and he would be very much surprised and exceedingly indignant with the maker, if he did not find it six o'clock also. Their chronometers are evidently in the same state, and have been doing the same thing; but what about their rifles? Given the condition of the one rifle, is it possible by any refinement of calculation to deduce that of the other? We feel at once that the bare supposition is ridiculous.

220. It is thus apparent that, as regards energy, structures are of two kinds. In one of these, the object sought is regularity of action, and the means employed, a stable arrangement of natural forces: while in the other, the end sought is freedom of action, and a sudden transmutation of energy, the means employed being an unstable arrangement of natural forces.

The one set of machines are characterized by their

calculability—the other by their incalculability. The one set, when at work, are not easily put wrong, while the other set are characterized by great delicacy of construction.

An Animal is a delicately-constructed Machine.

221. But perhaps the reader may object to our use of the rifle as an illustration.

For although it is undoubtedly a delicately-constructed machine, yet a rifle does not represent the same surpassing delicacy as that, for instance, which characterizes an egg balanced on its longer axis. Even if at full cock, and with a hair trigger, we may be perfectly certain it will not go off of its own accord. Although its object is to produce a sudden and violent transmutation of energy, yet this requires to be preceded by the application of an amount of energy, however small, to the trigger, and if this be not spent upon the rifle, it will not go off. There is, no doubt, delicacy of construction, but this has not risen to the height of incalculability, and it is only when in the hands of the sportsman that it becomes a machine upon the condition of which we cannot calculate.

Now, in making this remark, we define the position of the sportsman himself in the Universe of Energy.

The rifle is delicately constructed, but not surpassingly so; but sportsman and rifle, together, form a machine of surpassing delicacy, *ergo* the sportsman himself is such a machine. We thus begin to perceive that a human being, or indeed an animal of any kind, is in truth a machine of a delicacy that is practically infinite, the condition or motions of which we are utterly unable to predict.

In truth, is there not a transparent absurdity in the very thought that a man may become able to calculate his own movements, or even those of his fellow?

Life is like the Commander of an Army.

222. Let us now introduce another analogy—let us suppose that a war is being carried on by a vast army, at the head of which there is a very great commander. Now, this commander knows too well to expose his person; in truth, he is never seen by any of his subordinates. He remains at work in a well-guarded room, from which telegraphic wires lead to the headquarters of the various divisions. He can thus, by means of these wires, transmit his orders to the generals of these divisions, and by the same means receive back information as to the condition of each.

Thus his headquarters become a centre, into which all information is poured, and out of which all commands are issued.

Now, that mysterious thing called life, about the nature of which we know so little, is probably not unlike such a commander. Life is not a bully, who swaggers out into the open universe, upsetting the laws of energy in all directions, but rather a consummate strategist, who, sitting in his secret chamber, before his wires, directs the movements of a great army.*

223. Let us next suppose that our imaginary army is in rapid march, and let us try to find out the cause of this movement. We find that, in the first place, orders to march have been issued to the troops under them by the commanders of each regiment. In the next place, we learn that staff officers, attached to the generals of the various divisions, have conveyed these orders to the regimental commanders; and, finally, we learn that the order to march has been telegraphed from headquarters to these various generals.

Descending now to ourselves, it is probably somewhere in the mysterious and well-guarded brain-chamber that the delicate directive touch is given which determines our movements. This chamber forms, as it were, the headquarters of the general in command, who is so well withdrawn as to be absolutely invisible to all his subordinates.

224. Joule, Carpenter, and Mayer were at an early period aware of the restrictions under which animals are placed by the laws of energy, and in virtue of which the power of an animal, as far as energy is concerned, is not creative, but only directive. It was soon that, in order

* See an article on "The Position of Life," by the author of this work, in conjunction with Mr. J. N. Lockyer, "Macmillan's Magazine," September, 1868; also a lecture on "The Recent Developments of Cosmical Physics," by the author of this work.

to do work, an animal must be fed; and, even at a still earlier period, Count Rumford remarked that a ton of hay will be administered more economically by feeding a horse with it, and then getting work out of the horse, than by burning it as fuel in an engine.

225. In this chapter, the same line of thought has been carried out a little further. We have seen that life is associated with delicately-constructed machines, so that whenever a transmutation of energy is brought about by a living being, could we trace the event back, we should find that the physical antecedent was probably a much less transmutation, while again the antecedent of this would probably be found still less, and so on, as far as we could trace it.

226. But with all this, we do not pretend to have discovered the true nature of life itself, or even the true nature of its relation to the material universe.

What we have ventured is the assertion that, as far as we can judge, life is always associated with machinery of a certain kind, in virtue of which an extremely delicate directive touch is ultimately magnified into a very considerable transmutation of energy. Indeed, we can hardly imagine the freedom of motion implied in life to exist apart from machinery possessed of very great delicacy of construction.

In fine, we have not succeeded in solving the problem as to the true nature of life, but have only driven the difficulty into a borderland of thick darkness, into which the light of knowledge has not yet been able to penetrate.

Organized Tissues are subject to Decay.

227. We have thus learned two things, for, in the first place, we have learned that life is associated with delicacy of construction, and in the next (Art. 220), that delicacy of construction implies an unstable arrangement of natural forces. We have now to remark that the particular force which is thus used by living beings is chemical affinity. Our bodies are, in truth, examples of an unstable arrangement of chemical forces, and the materials which composed them, if not liable to sudden explosion, like fulminating powder, are yet pre-eminently the subjects of decay.

228. Now, this is more than a mere general statement; it is a truth that admits of degrees, and in virtue of which those parts of our bodies which have, during life, the noblest and most delicate office to perform, are the very first to perish when life is extinct.

> "Oh! o'er the eye death most exerts his might,
> And hurls the spirit from her throne of light;
> Sinks these blue orbs in their long last eclipse,
> But spares as yet the charm around the lips."

So speaks the poet, and we have here an aspect of things in which the lament of the poet becomes the true interpretation of nature.

Difference between Animals and Inanimate Machines.

220. We are now able to recognize the difference between the relations to energy of a living being, such as man, and a machine, such as a steam-engine.

There are many points in common between the two. Both require to be fed, and in both there is the transmutation of the energy of chemical separation implied in fuel and food into that of heat and visible motion.

But while the one—the engine—requires for its maintenance only carbon, or some other variety of chemical separation, the other—the living being—demands to be supplied with organized tissue. In fact, that delicacy of construction which is so essential to our well-being, is not something which we can elaborate internally in our own frames—all that we can do is to appropriate and assimilate that which comes to us from without; it is already present in the food which we eat.

Ultimate Dependence of Life upon the Sun.

230. We have already (Art. 203) been led to recognize the sun as the ultimate material source of all the energy which we possess, and we must now regard him as the source likewise of all our delicacy of construction. It requires the energy of his high temperature rays so to wield and manipulate the powerful forces of chemical affinity; so to balance these various forces against each

other, as to produce in the vegetable something which will afford our frames, not only energy, but also delicacy of construction.

Low temperature heat would be utterly unable to accomplish this; it consists of ethereal vibrations which are not sufficiently rapid, and of waves that are not sufficiently short, for the purpose of shaking asunder the constituents of compound molecules.

231. It thus appears that animals are, in more ways than one, pensioners upon the sun's bounty; and those instances, which at first sight appear to be exceptions, will, if studied sufficiently, only serve to confirm the rule.

Thus the recent researches of Dr. Carpenter and Professor Wyville Thomson have disclosed to us the existence of minute living beings in the deepest parts of the ocean, into which we may be almost sure no solar ray can penetrate. How, then, do these minute creatures obtain that energy and delicacy of construction without which they cannot live? in other words, how are they fed?

Now, the same naturalists who discovered the existence of these creatures, have recently furnished us with a very probable explanation of the mystery. They think it highly probable that the whole ocean contains in it organic matter to a very small but yet perceptible extent, forming, as they express it, a sort of diluted soup, which thus becomes the food of these minute creatures.

232. In conclusion, we are dependent upon the sun and centre of our system, not only for the mere energy of our

frames, but also for our delicacy of construction—the future of our race depends upon the sun's future. But we have seen that the sun must have had a beginning, and that he will have an end.

We are thus induced to generalize still further, and regard, not only our own system, but the whole material universe when viewed with respect to serviceable energy, as essentially evanescent, and as embracing a succession of physical events which cannot go on for ever as they are.

But here at length we come to matters beyond our grasp; for physical science cannot inform us what must have been before the beginning, nor yet can it tell us what will take place after the end.

INDEX.

A.

Absorbed Heat. Arts. 123-131, pp. 89-93
——— Art. 178, p. 128
——— in its two Forms. Arts. 149-162, pp. 105-118
Action and Reaction, Equal and Opposite. Art. 12, p. 8
——— Chemical, accompanied by Change of Condition. Art. 107, p. 121
Activity of Molecules. Arts. 10, 11, p. 7
Air and Water in Motion. Art. 209, p. 147
Advantages of Position. Art. 37, p. 26
Affinity, Chemical, force of. Arts. 70, 71, p. 53
——— Electricity probably allied to. Art. 84, p. 65
Analogy between Heat and Sound. Art. 57, p. 42
——— Hot and a Sounding Body. Art. 162, p. 118
Ancient Ideas not Prolific. Arts. 187, 188, p. 135
Animal a Delicately-constructed Machine. Art. 221, p. 160
Animals and Inanimate Machines, Difference between. Art. 229, p. 165
Arguments derived from Rumford's and Davy's Experiments. Arts. 53-55, p. 39
Aristotle on a Medium. Art. 186, p. 134
Army, Life like the Commander of an. Arts. 222-226, p. 171
Atmosphere, Resistance and Buoyancy of, disregarded. Art. 30, p. 20
Atoms and Molecules Defined. Arts. 68, 69, p. 51
——— Democritus on. Art. 185, p. 133
Atomic and Molecular Force, Remarks on. Arts. 72-78, p. 51
——— Forces, how influenced by Heat. Art. 76, p. 58
——— or Chemical Separation. Art. 111, p. 80
Attraction of Currents. Art. 173, p. 124

B.

Backward and Forward Motion, Heat a. Arts. 56, 57, pp. 41, 42
Bacon on Heat. Art. 190, p. 137
Bacon's Remarks. Art. 185, p. 134
Battery Current, Direction of. Arts. 94, 95, p. 71
—— Decomposition by the. Art. 177, p. 127
—— Poles of a. Art. 92, p. 71
—— Voltaic, the. Art. 169, 170, p. 123
Buoyancy and Resistance of Atmosphere disregarded. Art. 30, p. 20

C.

Carnot on Power of Heat. Art. 149, p. 106
Change into Heat of Mechanical Energy. Cap. 2, Arts. 31-63, pp. 23-47
—— of State. Art. 157, p. 112
—— Condition accompanies Chemical Action. Art. 167, p. 121
Chemical Action accompanied by Change of Condition. Art. 167, p. 121
—— Affinity, Force of. Arts. 70, 71, p. 53
—— Electricity probably allied to. Art. 84, p. 64
—— Effect of Current. Art. 99, p. 74
—— Instability. Art. 215, p. 156
—— or Atomic Separation. Art. 111, p. 80
—— Separation. Art. 159, p. 114
—— Arts. 163-170, pp. 118-123
—— Art. 177, p. 127
—— Arts. 179-181, p. 128
Cholera a Low Level Disease. Art. 6, p. 4
Coal. Art. 197, p. 143
Cohesion, Force of. Art. 8, p. 6
—— Arts. 68, 69, p. 51
Commander of an Army, Life is like the. Arts. 222-226, p. 171
Condition, Change of, accompanies Chemical Action. Art. 167, p. 121
Conditions of Equilibrium. Art. 44, p. 34
Conductors and Nonconductors. Art. 80, p. 61
Connection between Energies and Forces of Nature. Art. 61, p. 49
Conservation, Law of. Arts. 115-120, pp. 82, 83
—— Theory of. Art. 194, p. 140
Cross-bow, a bent. Art. 36, p. 25
Current, Chemical Effect of. Art. 99, p. 74
—— Heating Effect of. Art. 98, p. 73
—— Induction of. Art. 102-105, p. 75
—— Magnetic Effect of. Arts. 96, 97, p. 72
—— of Electricity. Arts. 140-143, p. 99

INDEX. 171

Current of Electricity. Art. 172, p. 124
Currents, Attraction and Repulsion of. Art. 100, p. 74
———————————————————— Art. 173, p. 124

D.

Davy's Experiments. Arts. 49-51, p. 38
Decay, Organized Tissues subject to. Arts. 227, 228, p. 164
Decomposition by the Battery. Art. 177, p. 127
Definition of Energy. Art. 10, p. 13
————— Molecules and Atoms. Arts. 68, 69, p. 51
————— Velocity. Art. 25, p. 16
————— Work. Art. 23, p. 15
Democritus on Atoms. Art. 185, p. 139
Descartes on a Medium. Art. 169, p. 136
Description of Electrical Current. Arts. 91, 92, p. 69
Difference between an Animate and Inanimate Machine. Art. 229, p. 165
Direction of Battery Current. Arts. 94, 95, p. 71
Directness of Motion, Energy Independent of. Art. 31, p. 21
Dissociation, Temperature of. Art. 159, p. 115
Diseases caused by Organic Germs. Art. 5, p. 3
Dissipation of Energy. Cap. 5, Arts. 182-210, pp. 131-152

E.

Earth, Falling off in Rotative Energy of. Art. 134, p. 95
——— Motions on the, Absorbed Heat in. Arts. 123-131, p. 88
——— The Air Engine. Art. 154, p. 108
Effect, Chemical, of Current. Art. 99, p. 74
——— Heating, of Current. Art. 98, p. 73
Effects, Magnetic, of Current. Arts. 96, 97, p. 72
Egg, a Balanced. Arts. 212, 213, pp. 154, 155
Elastic Forces. Art. 67, p. 50
Electric Current described, Arts 91, 92, p. 69
——— Induction. Arts. 87, 88, page 65
——— Machine. Art. 86, p. 65
——————— Arts. 138, 139, p. 98
Electrical Condition of the Poles. Art. 92, p. 71
——— Hypothesis. Art. 83, p. 63
——— Separation. Art. 112, p. 81
——————— Arts. 138, 139, p. 98
——————— Art. 160, p. 115
——————— Art. 168, p. 122
——————— Arts. 171, 172, p. 124
Electricity, a Current of. Arts. 140-143, p. 99

Electricity, a Current of. Art. 172, p. 124
——— in Motion. Art. 113, p. 81
——————— Art. 161, p. 116
——————— Arts. 169, 170, p. 123
——————— Arts. 173–177, pp. 124–127
——— its Properties. Arts. 79–105, pp. 60–76
——— List of Substances which develop it. Art. 85, p. 61
——— Magnetic. Arts. 144–147, p. 103
——— only produced when Heterogeneous Bodies are rubbed. Art. 84, p. 61
——— probably allied to Chemical Affinity. Art. 85, p. 61
——— remarks on. Arts. 79, 80, p. 60
——— two kinds of. Art. 81, p. 62
——————— always developed together. Art. 82, p. 61
Energies and Forces of Nature. Cap. 3, Arts. 64–107, pp. 48–78.
——— of Nature enumerated. Arts. 107–114, p. 78–81
——— Natural, and their Sources. Art. 196, p. 143
——————— chiefly from the Sun. Art. 203, p. 147
Energy, a Machine merely Transmutes it. Art. 42, p. 30
——— and Velocity, Relation between. Arts. 23–33, pp. 16–21
——— converted into less useful Form by Friction. Art. 46, p. 35
——————————————————— Percussion. Art. 47, p. 36
——— Definition of. Art. 19, p. 13
——— Dissipation of. Cap. 6, Arts. 182–210, pp. 131–152
——— Heating Effects proportional to. Art. 58, p. 43
——— Heraclitus on. Art. 184, p. 133
——— Independent of Directness of Motion. Art. 31, p. 21
——— Mechanical, and its Change into Heat. Cap. 2, Arts. 34–36, pp. 23–47
——— not simply proportional to Velocity. Arts. 21, 22, p. 14
——— of Position. Arts. 34–37, p. 23
——————— Arts. 108, 109, p. 79
——————— Arts. 121, 122, p. 87
——— of Visible Motion. Art. 107, p. 78
——————— Arts. 121–147, pp. 87–103
——————— Arts. 148, 149, p. 105
——— possessed by a Rifle Ball. Art. 18, p. 13
——— Problems allied to. Arts. 182, 183, p. 131
——— proportional to Mass. Art. 20, p. 14
——————— Square of Velocity. Art. 28, p. 12
——— Radiant. Art. 114, p. 81
——————— Art. 176–181, p. 128
——— the Power of doing Work. Art. 23, p. 15
——— There are other varieties of. Art. 62, p. 47
——— Tidal. Art. 206, p. 146
——— Transmutation of. Cap 4, Arts. 121–187, pp. 87–129
——— Visible, Transmutations of. Arts. 38–41, pp. 27, 28

INDEX.

Energy, Visible, of Position. Art. 148, p. 105
——— What is it? Cap. I, Art. 1, p. 1
Engine, the Heat. Art. 149, p. 105
——— the Earth an. Art. 154, p. 108
Engines, Law of Working of Heat. Arts. 150-152, p. 106
——— Remarks on. Art. 154, p. 108
Enumeration of Energies of Nature. Arts. 107-114, pp. 78-81
——— Forces of Matter. Arts. 65-78, pp. 48-55
Equal and Opposite, Action and Reaction. Art. 2, p. 3
Equilibrium, Conditions of. Art. 44, p. 24
——— twofold Nature of. Art. 212, p. 154
Equivalent, Mechanical, of Heat. Arts. 58-63, pp. 43-47
Examples. Art. 29, p. 20
Existence a Continued Fight. Art. 3, p. 3
Experiments by Davy. Arts. 49-51, p. 38
——— Joule. Arts. 59-61, p. 44
——— Peltier. Arts. 176, p. 126
——— Rumford. Art. 52, p. 39

F.

Fate, Probable, of the Universe. Arts. 209, 210, p. 152
Falling Stone, Illustration of a. Arts. 15, 16, p. 11
Fire, an ordinary. Art. 153, p. 108
Fluids, Friction of. Art. 59, p. 44
Food. Art. 199, p. 145
Force of Chemical Affinity. Arts. 70, 71, p. 52
——— Cohesion. Art. 8, p. 6
——— Arts. 68, 69, p. 51
Forces and Energies of Nature. Cap. 3, Arts. 64-107, pp. 48-78
——— other, besides Gravity. Arts. 32, 33, p. 21
Forward and Backward Motion, Heat a. Arts. 56, 57, pp. 41, 42
Freezing Point of Water lowered by Pressure. Art. 150, p. 110
Friction and Percussion, what they do. Arts. 20-48, pp. 35-37
——— converts Energy into less useful Form. Art. 40, p. 35
——— of Fluids. Art. 64, p. 44
Fuel, embracing Wood and Coal. Art. 107, p. 143
Functions of a Machine. Arts. 42, 43, pp. 30-32

G.

Galileo defined Principles of Virtual Velocities. Art. 44, p. 33
——— true Function of a Machine. Art. 44, p. 30
Galvanometer, the. Art. 96, p. 72
Goldfish, vessel of. Art. 13, p. 9

Gravitation a Weak Force. Art. 66, p. 50
———— its Law of Action. Art. 65, p. 48
Gravity, other Forces besides. Arts. 32, 33, p. 21
Grove on Conservation. Art. 194, p. 140

H

Head, a, of Water. Art. 35, p. 24
———— Art. 200, p. 146
Heat, Absorbed. Art. 178, p. 128
—— a Backward and Forward Motion. Arts. 66-69, pp. 41, 42
—— a species of Motion. Arts. 49-56, pp. 48, 39
—— (a resisting body). Arts. 174, 175, p. 125
—— analogy between, and Sound. Art. 57, p. 42
—— appears when Friction and Percussion destroy Motion. Art. 18, p. 37
—— Bacon on. Art. 190, p. 137
—— Change into, of Mechanical Energy. Cap. 2, Arts. 34-63, 23-47
—— Engine, Energy of Visible Motion in the. Art. 149, p. 150
———————— Law of Working of. Arts. 150-152, p. 106
—— Mechanical Equivalent of. Arts. 58-63, pp. 34-47
—— Motion. Art. 110, p. 50
—— Origin of the Sun's. Arts. 207, 208, p. 150
—— Radiant. Art. 162, p. 117
—— Unit, value of. Art. 62, p. 46
Heated Substance not in Motion as a whole. Art. 56, p. 41
Heating Effect of Current. Art. 98, p. 73
Heating Effects proportional to Energy. Art. 98, p. 73
Helmholtz and Thomson on the Origin of the Sun's Heat. Art. 207, p. 151
Heraclitus on Energy. Art. 184, p. 133
Heterogeneous Bodies only produce Electricity when rubbed. Art. 84, p. 64
———————— Metals Soldered together. Art. 168, p. 122
High Temperature Heat, the Sun the Source of. Art. 204, p. 148
Historical Sketch. Cap. 5, Arts. 182-210, pp. 131-152
Hot and Sounding Body, analogy between. Art. 162, p. 118
Huyghens on a Medium. Art. 189, p. 136
Hydrostatic Press. Art. 43, p. 32
Hypothesis, Electrical. Art. 89, p. 63

L

Ice Melted by Friction. Art. 123, p. 88
Ideas of Ancients not Prolific. Arts. 187, 188, p. 135

INDEX. 175

Ignorance of Individuals. Arts. 1–4, p. 1
Impossibility of Perpetual Light. Art. 245, p. 149
——————— seeing Molecules. Art. 11, p. 8
Inanimate Machines, difference between Animals and. Art. 229. p. 165
Inclined Plane, Velocity in the. Arts. 40, 41, p. 29
——————————————————— Art. 45, p. 34
Individuals, Ignorance of. Arts. 1–4, p. 1
Induction, Electric. Arts. 87, 88, p. 65
——————— of Currents. Arts. 102–105, p. 75
Inorganic Molecule, an. Art. 7, p. 5
——————— World, the. Arts. 5, 6, p. 3
Instability, Chemical. Art. 215, p. 156
——————— Mechanical. Arts. 213, 214, p. 155

J.

Jevons, Prof. S., on Coal Supply. Art. 199, pp. 144, 145
Joule's Experiments. Arts. 59–61, p. 41

K.

Kilogramme, Descending. Art. 39, p. 28
——————— shot Upwards. Art. 26, 27, p. 17
———————————————— Art. 38, p. 27

L.

Latent Heat of Steam. Art. 74, p. 57
——————— Water. Art. 73, p. 56
Law of Action of Gravitation. Art. 65, p. 49
——— Conservation. Arts. 115–120, pp. 82, 83
——— Working of Heat Engines. Arts. 150–152, p. 106
Leaves of Plants. Arts. 179–181, p. 128
Lever, Illustration of. Art. 45, p. 34
Leyden Jar. Arts. 80, 90, p. 67
Life like the Commander of an Army. Arts. 222–226, p. 171
——— the Position of. Cap. 6, Arts. 211–232, pp. 154–165
——— true Nature of, not discovered. Art. 224, p. 163
——— Ultimate Dependence of, on the Sun. Arts. 230–232, p. 165
Light, Perpetual, Impossible. Art. 205, p. 249
——— Radiant. Art. 162, p. 117
List of Substances which develop Electricity. Art. 85, p. 64
Low Level Disease, Cholera a. Art. 6, p. 3

M.

Machine, Animal is a Delicately constructed. Art. 221, p. 160
——— does not Create. Art. 44, p. 34
——— Electric. Art. 86, p. 65
——————— Arts. 138, 139, p. 98
——— Functions of a. Arts. 42, 43, pp. 30-32
————————— described by Galileo. Art. 41, p. 33
——— merely transmutes Energy. Art. 42, p. 30
Machines of two kinds. Arts. 216-220, p. 157
Magnet, Attraction and Repulsion of. Art. 101, p. 76
Magnetic Effects of Current. Arts. 96, 97, p. 72
Magneto-Electricity. Arts. 144-147, p. 103
Mass, Energy Proportional to. Art. 20, p. 14
Meyer on Theory of Conservation. Art. 191, p. 140
——— Tides. Art. 133, p. 91
Mechanical Energy and its Change into Heat. Cap. 2, Arts. 34-63, pp. 23-47
——————— Equivalent of Heat. Arts. 58-63, pp. 45-47
——————— Instability. Arts. 213, 214, p. 155
Medium, Aristotle on a. Art. 186, p. 134
——— Descartes on a. Art. 189, p. 136
——— Huyghens on a. Art. 189, p. 136
——— Newton on a. Art. 189, p. 136
Metallic Precipitates. Arts. 165, 166, p. 120
Metals, soldering together of Heterogeneous. Art. 168, p. 122
Molecules, Activity of. Arts. 10, 11, p. 7
——— and Atoms Defined. Arts. 68, 69, p. 51
Molecular and Atomic Force, remarks on. Arts. 72-78, p. 55
——— Forces, Strength of. Art. 76, p. 57
————————— Impossible to become directly acquainted with. Art. 11, p. 8
——— Separation. Art. 110, p. 80
Motion, Air and Water in. Art. 203, p. 147
——— Electricity in. Art. 107, p. 88
————————— Art. 161, p. 116
————————— Arts. 169, 170, p. 123
——— Energy Independent of Direction of. Art. 31, p. 21
——————— of Visible. Arts. 121-147, pp. 87-103
————————— Arts. 148, 149, p. 105
——— Heat a Forward and Backward. Arts. 56, 57, pp. 41, 42
——————— a species of. Arts. 49-55, pp. 38, 39
——— Visible. Arts. 171-173, p. 124
——————— Energy in. Art. 113, p. 81
Motions on the Earth, Absorbed Heat in. Arts. 131, 132, p. 88
——— Planetary. Arts. 132-137, p. 93

N.

Native Sulphur, &c. Art. 102, p. 147
Nature, Energies of, Enumerated. Arts. 107-114, pp. 78-81
——— Forces and Energies of. Cap. 3, Arts. 64-107, pp. 48-78
——— of, Enumerated. Arts. 65-78, pp. 48-55
——— of Proof of Law of Conservation. Arts. 117-120, p. 83
Natural Energies chiefly from Sun. Art. 203, p. 147
——— and their Sources. Art. 196, p. 143
Newton on a Medium. Art. 189, p. 136
Nonconductors and Conductors. Art. 80, p. 61

O.

Opposite and Equal, Action and Reaction. Art. 12, p. 6
Organic and Inorganic Worlds. Art. 4, p. 3
——— Germs, Diseases caused by. Art. 5, p. 3
——— World, the. Arts. 7-9, p. 5
Organized Tissues subject to Decay. Arts. 227, 228, p. 164
Origin of the Sun's Heat. Arts. 207, 208, p. 150
Other Varieties of Energy. Art. 62, p. 47

P.

Peltier's Experiment. Art. 176, p. 126
Percussion converts Energy into less useful Form. Art. 47, p. 38
——— what Friction and, do. Arts. 26-48, pp. 35-37
Perpetual Light Impossible. Art. 205, p. 149
——— Motion. Art. 193, p. 130
Pith Ball, experiments with. Art. 81, p. 62
Planetary Motions, Absorbed Heat in. Arts. 132-137, p. 93
Plants, leaves of. Arts. 179-181, p. 128
Poles, Electrical Condition of. Art. 93, p. 7
——— of a Battery, the. Art. 92, p. 71
Position, Advantage of. Art. 97, p. 26
——— Energy of. Art. 34-37, pp. 23-26
——— Art. 121, 122, p. 87
——— the, of Life. Cap. 6, Arts. 211-232, pp. 154-165
——— Visible Energy of. Arts. 108, 109, p. 79
——— Art. 148, p. 105
Precipitates, Metallic. Arts. 165, 166, p. 120
Preliminary Remarks. Art. 211, p. 154
Pressure lowers Freezing Point of Water. Art. 156, p. 110
Prince Rupert's Drops. Art. 158, p. 114

Principles of Virtual Velocities. Arts. 44, 45, pp. 33, 34
———————————————————— Art. 191, p. 147
Probable Fate of Universe. Arts. 209, 210, p. 152
Problems allied to Energy. Arts. 182, 183, p. 131
Properties of Electricity. Arts. 99-105, pp. 60-75

R.

Radiant Energy. Art. 114, p. 81
———————— Art. 176, p. 128
———————— Light and Heat. Art. 162, p. 117
Reaction and Action, Equal and Opposite. Arts. 12-16, p. 8
Relation between Velocity and Energy. Arts. 25-33, pp. 10-21
Remarks, Bacon's. Art. 185, p. 134
———————— on Electricity. Arts. 79, 80, p. 60
———————— Engines. Art. 155, p. 109
———————— Molecular and Atomic Forces. Arts. 72-78, p. 55
———————— Whewell's. Art. 186, p. 134
Repulsion and Attraction of Currents. Art. 100, p. 74
———————— of Magnets. Art. 101, p. 75
Resistance and Buoyancy of Atmosphere disregarded. Art. 30, p. 20
Rifle Ball possesses Energy. Art. 18, p. 13
———— Further Considered. Art. 17, p. 12
———— Illustration of. Arts. 13, 14, p. 9
Rise of True Conceptions regarding Work. Art. 192, p. 133
Rule for Measuring Work. Art. 24, p. 16
Rumford's Experiments. Art. 52, p. 39

S.

Scott, Sir W., on Perpetual Light. Art. 204, p. 148
Separation, Atomic or Chemical. Art. 111, p. 80
———————— Chemical. Art. 159, p. 114
———————————————— Arts. 163-170, pp. 118-123
———————————————— Arts. 177, p. 127
———————————————— Arts. 170-181, p. 128
———————— Electrical. Art. 112, p. 81
———————————————— Arts. 138, 139, p. 98
———————————————— Art. 160, p. 115
———————————————— Art. 168, p. 122
———————————————— Arts. 171, 172, p. 124
———————— Molecular. Art. 110, p. 80
Set of Pulleys. Art. 42, p. 30
Sketch, Historical. Cap. 5, Arts. 182-210, pp. 131-152
Soldering together of Heterogeneous Metals. Art. 168, p. 122
Sound and Heat, Analogy between. Art. 57, p. 42

Sounding and Hot Body, Analogy between. Art. 162, p. 118
Sources of Natural Energies. Art. 196, p. 143
Square of Velocity, Energy proportional to. Art. 28, p. 19
Stable and Unstable Equilibrium. Art. 212, p. 154
Statement of Law of Conservation. Art. 115, 116, p. 83
Steam, Latent Heat of. Art. 74, p. 67
Stone, a, high up. Art. 34, p. 23
Strength of Molecular Forces. Art. 75, p. 57
Substances, List of, which develop Electricity. Art. 85, p. 64
Sulphur, Native. Art. 202, p. 147
Sun a Source of High Temperature Heat. Art. 201, p. 145
Sun Heat, Origin of the. Arts. 207, 208, p. 150
—— Natural Energies chiefly from. Art. 213, p. 147
—— no exception. Art. 208, p. 150
—— Ultimate dependence of Life on the. Arts. 250-252, p. 165
Survey of Organic and Inorganic Worlds. Art. 4, p. 3

T.

Tait, Professor, on Native Sulphur, &c. Art. 202, p. 147
Temperature of Dissassociation. Art. 159, p. 115
Theory, the, of Conversation. Art. 194, p. 140
Thermo-Electricity. Art. 161, p. 110
Thermopile, the. Art. 161, p. 117
Thompson, Sir William, and Helmholtz, theory of Sun's Heat. Art. 207, p. 151
———————————— on lowering Freezing Point of Water by Pressure, Art. 156, pp. 110, 111
———————————— Size of Molecules. Art. 8, p. 6
Tidal Energy. Art. 201, p. 146
Tissues, Organised, are subject to Decay. Arts. 227, 228, p. 164
Tourmalines, &c., Heated. Art. 160, p. 115
Transmutation of Energy. Cap. 4, Arts. 121-181, pp. 87-128
———————————— Visible Energy. Arts. 38-41, pp. 27, 28
True Conceptions, Rise of, regarding Work. Art. 192, p. 138
—— Functions of a Machine defined by Galileo. Art. 11, p. 11
Two Forms of Absorbed Heat. Arts. 149-162, pp. 105-118
—— Kinds of Electricity. Art. 81, p. 62
———————————— always developed together. Art. 82, p. 63
———————————— Machines. Arts. 216-220, p. 157
Twofold Nature of Equilibrium. Art. 212, p. 154

U.

Ultimate Dependence of Life on the Sun. Arts. 230-232, p. 165
Universe, probable Fate of the. Arts. 209, 210, p. 152
Unstable and Stable Equilibrium. Art. 212, p. 154

V.

Value of Heat Unit. Art. 62, p. 46
Varieties, other, of Energy. Art. 63, p. 47
Velocities, principles of Virtual. Arts. 44, 45, pp. 33, 34
———————— Art. 191, p. 137
Velocity and Energy, relation between. Arts. 25–33, pp. 16–21
———————— Definition of. Art. 25, p. 16
———————— Energy not simply proportional to. Arts. 21, 22, p. 14
———————— in Inclined Plane. Arts. 40, 41, p. 28
———————— Square of Energy proportionate to. Art. 28, p. 19
Virtual Velocities, principles of. Arts. 44, 45, pp. 33, 34
———————— Art. 191, p. 137
Visible Energy, Transmutation of. Arts. 38–41, pp. 27, 29
———————— of Position. Arts. 108, 109, p. 79
———————— Art. 148, p. 105
Visible Motion. Arts. 171–173, p. 124
———————— Energy of. Art. 107, p. 78
———————— Arts. 121–147, pp. 87–103
———————— Arts. 148, 149, p. 105
Voltaic Battery, the. Arts. 169, 170, p. 123

W.

Watch, a, wound up. Art. 36, p. 25
Water and Air in Motion. Art. 203, p. 147
——— A Head of. Art. 55, p. 24
——————— Art. 200, p. 146
——— Freezing Point of. Arts. 118, 119, p. 85
————————— lowered by Pressure. Art. 150, p. 110
——— Latent Heat of. Art. 74, p. 56
Watts' improvements in Steam Engine. Art. 192, p. 138
What Friction and Percussion do. Arts. 46–48, pp. 35–37
——— is Energy? Cap. 1, Art. 1. p. 1
Whewell's Remarks. Art. 186, p. 134
Whole of Heated Substance not in Motion. Art. 56, p. 45
Wild's Machines for obtaining Electricity. Arts. 144, 145, pp. 103, 104
Wood. Art. 197, p. 143
Work, Definition of. Art. 23, p. 15
——— How to Measure. Art. 23, p. 15
——— Rise of True Conceptions concerning. Art. 192, p. 138
——— Rule for Measuring. Art. 24, p. 16
Working Heat Engine, Law of. Art. 150–152, p. 106

The International Scientific Series.

List of Authors and their Books.

THE INTERNATIONAL SCIENTIFIC SERIES.

The following is a List of the Works already published.

Third Edition.

THE FORMS OF WATER IN RAIN AND RIVERS, ICE AND GLACIERS. By J. Tyndall, LL.D., F.R.S. With 26 Illustrations. Crown 8vo. 5s.

"One of Professor Tyndall's best scientific treatises."—*Standard.*

"With the clearness and brilliancy of language which have won for him his fame, he considers the subject of ice, snow, and glaciers."—*Morning Post.*

"Before starting for Switzerland next summer every one should study 'The forms of water.'"—*Globe.*

"Eloquent and instructive in an eminent degree."—*British Quarterly.*

Second Edition.

PHYSICS AND POLITICS; or, Thoughts on the Application of the Principles of "Natural Selection" and "Inheritance" to Political Society. By **Walter Bagehot.** Crown 8vo. 4s.

"On the whole we can recommend the book as well deserving to be read by thoughtful students of politics."—*Saturday Review.*

"Able and ingenious."—*Spectator.*

"A work of really original and interesting speculation. Mr. Bagehot has undertaken to inquire what are the conditions which enable nations to enter on a course of progress and to continue in it."—*Guardian.*

Second Edition.

FOODS. By Dr. **Edward Smith.** Profusely Illustrated. 6s.

Second Edition.

MIND AND BODY: The Theories of their Relations. By **Alexander Bain,** LL.D., Professor of Logic at the University of Aberdeen. Four Illustrations. Crown 8vo. 4s.

THE STUDY OF SOCIOLOGY. By **Herbert Spencer.** Crown 8vo. 5s.

ANIMAL MECHANICS; or, Walking, Swimming, and Flying. By Dr. J. **Bell Pettigrew,** M.D., F.R.S. Crown 8vo. 125 Illustrations.

THE ANIMAL MACHINE; or, Aerial and Terrestrial Locomotion. By C. J. **Marey,** Professor of the College of France; Member of the Academy of Medicine, Paris. Crown 8vo. 117 Engravings.

RESPONSIBILITY IN MENTAL DISEASE. By Dr. **Henry Maudsley.** Crown 8vo.

LIST OF AUTHORS AND SUBJECTS OF THEIR BOOKS,
TO BE PUBLISHED IN THE
INTERNATIONAL SCIENTIFIC SERIES.

Dr. J. B. PETTIGREW, M.D., F.R.S.
Animal Mechanics; or, Walking, Swimming, and Flying.

Dr. HENRY MAUDSLEY.
Responsibility in Disease.

Prof. E. J. MAREY.
The Animal Frame.

Rev. M. J. BERKELEY, M.A., F.L.S., and M. COOKE, M.A., LL.D.
Fungi: their Nature, Influences, and Uses.

Prof. OSCAR SCHMIDT (Univ. of Strasburg).
The Theory of Descent and Darwinism.

Prof. W. KINGDOM CLIFFORD, M.A.
The First Principles of the exact Sciences explained to the non-mathematical.

Prof. T. H. HUXLEY, LL.D., F.R.S.
Bodily Motion and Consciousness.

Dr. W. B. CARPENTER, LL.D., F.R.S.
The Physical Geography of the Sea.

Prof. WILLIAM ODLING, F.R.S.
The New Chemistry.

Prof. SHELDON AMOS.
The Science of Law.

W. LAUDER LINDSAY, M.D., F.R.S.E.
Mind in the Lower Animals.

Sir JOHN LUBBOCK, Bart., F.R.S.
The Antiquity of Man.

Prof. W. T. THISELTON DYER, B.A., B.SC.
Form and Habit in Flowering Plants.

Mr. J. N. LOCKYER, F.R.S.
Spectrum Analysis.

Prof. MICHAEL FOSTER, M.D.
Protoplasm and the Cell Theory.

Prof. W. STANLEY JEVONS.
The Logic of Statistics.

Dr. H. CHARLTON BASTIAN, M.D., F.R.S.
The Brain as an Organ of Mind.

Prof. A. C. RAMSAY, LL.D., F.R.S.
Earth Sculpture; Hills, Valleys, Mountains, Plains, Rivers, Lakes; how they were Produced, and how they have been Destroyed.

Prof. RUDOLPH VIRCHOW (Univ. of Berlin).
Morbid Physiological Action.

Prof. CLAUDE BERNARD (Col. of France).
Physical and Metaphysical Phenomena of Life.

Prof. A. QUETELET (Brussels Acad. of Sciences).
Social Physics.

Prof. H. SAINTE CLAIRE DEVILLE.
An Introduction to General Chemistry.

Prof. WURTZ.
Atoms and the Atomic Theory.

Prof. DE QUATREFAGES.
The Negro Races.

Prof. LACAZE-DUTHIERS.
Zoology since Cuvier.

Prof. BERTHELOT.
Chemical Synthesis.

Prof. J. ROSENTHAL.
General Physiology of Muscles and Nerves.

Prof. JAMES D. DANA, M.A., LL.D.
On Cephalization; or, Head-Characters in the Gradation and Progress of Life.

Prof. S. W. JOHNSON, M.A.
On the Nutrition of Plants.

Prof. AUSTIN FLINT, Jr., M.D.
The Nervous System and its Relation to the Bodily Functions.

Prof. W. D. WHITNEY.
Modern Linguistic Science.

Prof. BERNSTEIN (University of Halle).
Physiology of the Senses.

Prof. FERDINAND COHN (Univ. of Breslau).
Thallophytes (Algae Lichens Fungi).

Prof. HERMANN (University of Zurich).
Respiration.

Prof. LEUCKART (University of Leipsic).
Outlines of Animal Organisation.

Prof. LIEBREICH (University of Berlin).
Outlines of Toxicology.

Prof. KUNDT (University of Strasburg).
On Sound.

Prof. LOMMEL (University of Erlangen).
Optics.

Prof. REES (University of Erlangen).
On Parasitic Plants.

Prof. STEINTHAL (University of Berlin).
Outlines of the Science of Language.

Prof. VOGEL (Polytechnic Acad. of Berlin).
The Chemical Effects of Light.

HENRY S. KING & CO., 65 CORNHILL, AND 12 PATERNOSTER ROW, LONDON.

Printed by William Moore & Co.

NOVEMBER, 1873.

A Classified Catalogue of Henry S. King & Co.'s Publications.

CONTENTS.

	PAGE		PAGE
HISTORY AND BIOGRAPHY	1	INDIA AND THE EAST	19
VOYAGES AND TRAVEL	5	BOOKS FOR THE YOUNG, &c.	21
SCIENCE	7	POETRY	24
ESSAYS, LECTURES, AND COLLECTED PAPERS	12	FICTION	26
MILITARY WORKS	15	THEOLOGICAL	31
		CORNHILL LIBRARY OF FICTION	36

HISTORY AND BIOGRAPHY.

THE NORMAN PEOPLE, AND THEIR EXISTING DESCENDANTS IN THE BRITISH DOMINIONS AND THE UNITED STATES OF AMERICA. One handsome vol. 8vo. Price 21s. [*In the Press.*

This work is the result of many years of research into the history of the Norman race in England. It is generally supposed to have become extinct; but careful study has shown that it exists and forms a large part of the English people. In the course of the work the early history of the whole aristocracy is revised, reconstructed, and very many thousands of families are shown to be Norman which have never before been accounted for.

A MEMOIR OF THE LATE REVEREND DR. ROWLAND WILLIAMS, With selections from his Note-books and Correspondence. Edited by **Mrs. Rowland Williams.** With a Photographic Portrait. [*In the Press.*

THE RUSSIANS IN CENTRAL ASIA. A Critical Examination, down to the present time, of the Geography and History of Central Asia. By **Baron F. Von Hellwald**, Member of the Geographical Societies of Paris, Geneva, Vienna, &c., &c. Translated by **Lieut.-Col. Theodore Wirgman, LL.B.**, late 6th Inniskilling Dragoons; formerly of the Austrian Service; Translator into English verse of Schiller's "Wallenstein's Camp." [*Nearly ready.*

65, Cornhill; & 12, Paternoster Row, London.

HISTORY AND BIOGRAPHY—*continued*.

THE GOVERNMENT OF THE NATIONAL DEFENCE. From the 30th June to the 31st October, 1870. The Plain Statement of a Member. By **Mons. Jules Favre.** 1 vol. Demy 8vo. 10s. 6d.

BOKHARA: ITS HISTORY AND CONQUEST. By Professor **Arminius Vámbéry**, of the University of Pesth, Author of "Travels in Central Asia," &c. Demy 8vo. Price 18s.

"We conclude with a cordial recommendation of this valuable book. In the present work his moderation, scholarship, insight, and occasionally very impressive style, have raised him to the dignity of an historian."—*Saturday Review.*

"Almost every page abounds with composition of peculiar merit, as well as with an account of some thrilling event more exciting than any to be found in an ordinary work of fiction."—*Morning Post.*

THE RELIGIOUS HISTORY OF IRELAND: PRIMITIVE, PAPAL, AND PROTESTANT; including the Evangelical Missions, Catholic Agitations, and Church Progress of the last half century. By **James Godkin**, Author of "Ireland, her Churches," &c. 1 vol. 8vo. Price 12s.

"For those who shun blue books, and yet desire some of the information they contain, these latter chapters on the statistics of the various religious denominations will be welcomed."—*Evening Standard.*

"Mr. Godkin writes with evident honesty, and the topic on which he writes is one about which an honest book is greatly wanted."—*Examiner.*

'ILÂM ÊN NÂS. Historical Tales and Anecdotes of the Times of the Early Khalifahs. Translated from the Arabic Originals. By **Mrs. Godfrey Clerk**, Author of "The Antipodes and Round the World." Crown 8vo. Price 7s.

"But there is a high tone about them, a love of justice, of truth and integrity, a sense of honour and manliness, and a simple devotion to religious duty, which however mistaken according to our lights, is deserving of every respect. The translation is the work of a lady, and a very excellent and scholar-like translation it is, clearly and pleasantly written, and illustrated and explained by copious notes, indicating considerable learning and research."—*Saturday Review.*
"Those who like stories full of the genuine colour and fragrance of the East, should by all means read Mrs. Godfrey Clerk's volume."—*Spectator.*
"As full of valuable information as it is of amusing incident."—*Evening Standard.*

ECHOES OF A FAMOUS YEAR. By **Harriet Parr**, Author of "The Life of Jeanne d'Arc," "In the Silver Age," &c. Crown 8vo. 8s. 6d.

"A graceful and touching, as well as truthful account of the Franco-Prussian War. Those who are in the habit of reading books to children will find this at once instructive and delightful."—*Public Opinion.*

"Miss Parr has the great gift of charming simplicity of style; and if children are not interested in her book, many of their seniors will be."—*British Quarterly Review.*

65, Cornhill; & 12, Paternoster Row, London.

HISTORY AND BIOGRAPHY—*continued*.

ALEXIS DE TOCQUEVILLE. Correspondence and Conversations with NASSAU W. SENIOR from 1833 to 1859. Edited by **Mrs. M. C. M. Simpson**. In 2 vols., large post 8vo. 21*s*.

"Another of those interesting journals in which Mr. Senior has, as it were, crystallised the sayings of some of those many remarkable men with whom he came in contact."—*Morning Post*.

"A book replete with knowledge and thought."—*Quarterly Review*.
"An extremely interesting book."—*Saturday Review*.

JOURNALS KEPT IN FRANCE AND ITALY. From 1848 to 1852. With a Sketch of the Revolution of 1848. By the late **Nassau William Senior**. Edited by his Daughter, **M. C. M. Simpson**. In 2 vols., post 8vo. 24*s*.

"The book has a genuine historical value."—*Saturday Review*.
"The present volume gives us conversations with some of the most prominent men in the political history of France and Italy... Mr. Senior has the art of inspiring all men with frankness, and of persuading them to put themselves unreservedly in his hands without fear of private circulation."—*Athenæum*.
"No better, more honest, and more readable view of the state of political society during the existence of the second Republic could well be looked for."—*Examiner*.

POLITICAL WOMEN. By **Sutherland Menzies**. 2 vols. Post 8vo. Price 24*s*.

"Has all the information of history, with all the interest that attaches to biography."—*Scotsman*.
"A graceful contribution to the lighter record of history."—*English Churchman*.

"No author could have stated the case more temperately than he has done, and few could have placed before the reader so graphically the story which had to be told."—*Leeds Mercury*.

SARA COLERIDGE, MEMOIR AND LETTERS OF. Edited by her **Daughters**. 2 vols. Crown 8vo. With 2 Portraits. Price 24*s*. Second Edition, Revised and Corrected.

"We have read these two volumes with genuine gratification."—*Hour*.
"We could have wished to give specimens of her very just, subtle, and concise criticisms on authors of every sort and time —poets, moralists, historians, and philosophers. Sara Coleridge, as she is revealed, or rather reveals herself, in the correspondence, makes a brilliant addition to a brilliant family reputation."—*Saturday Review*.

"These charming volumes are attractive in two ways: first, as a memorial of a most amiable woman of high intellectual mark; and secondly, as rekindling recollections, and adding a little to our information regarding the life of Sara Coleridge's father, the poet and philosopher."—*Athenæum*.
"An acceptable record, and present an adequate image of a mind of singular beauty and no inconsiderable power."—*Examiner*.

PHANTASMION. A Fairy Romance. By **Sara Coleridge**.

[*In preparation.*

65, *Cornhill*; & 12, *Paternoster Row, London*.

HISTORY AND BIOGRAPHY—*continued*.

LEONORA CHRISTINA, MEMOIRS OF, Daughter of Christian IV. of Denmark: Written during her Imprisonment in the Blue Tower of the Royal Palace at Copenhagen, 1663—1685. Translated by F. E. Bunnett, Translator of Grimm's "Life of Michael Angelo," &c. With an Autotype Portrait of the Princess. Medium 8vo. 12s. 6d.

"A valuable addition to history."—*Daily News*.

"This remarkable autobiography, in which we gratefully recognise a valuable addition to the tragic romance of history."—*Spectator*.

THE LATE REV. F. W. ROBERTSON, M.A., LIFE AND LETTERS OF. Edited by Stopford Brooke, M.A., Chaplain in Ordinary to the Queen. In 2 vols., uniform with the Sermons. Price 7s. 6d. Library Edition, in demy 8vo, with Two Steel Portraits. 12s. A Popular Edition, in 1 vol. Price 6s.

NATHANIEL HAWTHORNE, A MEMOIR OF, with Stories now first published in this country. By H. A. Page. Large post 8vo. 7s. 6d.

"The Memoir is followed by a criticism of Hawthorne as a writer; and the criticism is, on the whole, very well written, and exhibits a discriminating enthusiasm for one of the most fascinating of novelists."—*Saturday Review*.

"Seldom has it been our lot to meet with a more appreciative delineation of character than this Memoir of Hawthorne."—*Morning Post*.

"He has done full justice to the fine character of the author of 'The Scarlet Letter.'"—*Standard*.

"A model of literary work of art."—*Edinburgh Courant*.

LIVES OF ENGLISH POPULAR LEADERS. No. 1.—STEPHEN LANGTON. By C. Edmund Maurice. Crown 8vo. 7s. 6d.

"Mr. Maurice has written a very interesting book, which may be read with equal pleasure and profit."—*Morning Post*.

"The volume contains many interesting details, including some important documents. It will amply repay those who read it, whether as a chapter of the constitutional history of England or as the life of a great Englishman."—*Spectator*.

CABINET PORTRAITS. BIOGRAPHICAL SKETCHES OF LIVING STATESMEN. By T. Wemyss Reid. 1 vol. crown 8vo. 7s. 6d.

"We have never met with a work which we can more unreservedly praise. The sketches are absolutely impartial."—*Athenæum*.

"We can heartily commend his work."—*Standard*.

"The 'Sketches of Statesmen' are drawn with a master hand."—*Yorkshire Post*.

VOYAGES AND TRAVEL.

ROUGH NOTES OF A VISIT TO BELGIUM, SEDAN, AND PARIS, In September, 1870—71. By **John Ashton**. Crown 8vo, bevelled boards. Price 3s. 6d.

This little volume derives its chief interest from the accurate descriptions of the scenes visited during the recent struggle on the Continent.

THE ALPS OF ARABIA; or, Travels through Egypt, Sinai, Arabia, and the Holy Land. By **William Charles Maughan**. 1 vol. Demy 8vo, with Map. Price 10s. 6d.

A volume of simple "impressions de voyage"—but written in pleasant and interesting style.

THE MISHMEE HILLS: an Account of a Journey made in an Attempt to Penetrate Tibet from Assam, to open New Routes for Commerce. By **T. T. Cooper**, author of "The Travels of a Pioneer of Commerce." Demy 8vo. Illustrated.

THE PEARL OF THE ANTILLES; The Artist in Cuba. By **Walter Goodman**. Crown 8vo. 7s. 6d.

"A good-sized volume, delightfully vivid and picturesque. . . . Several chapters devoted to the characteristics of the people are exceedingly interesting and remarkable. . . . The whole book deserves the heartiest commendation . . . sparkling and amusing from beginning to end. Reading it is like rambling about with a companion who is content to loiter, observing everything, commenting upon everything, turning everything into a picture, with a cheerful flow of spirits, full of fun, but far above frivolity."—*Spectator*.

"He writes very lightly and pleasantly, and brightens his pages with a good deal of humour. His experiences were varied enough, and his book contains a series of vivid and miscellaneous sketches. We can recommend his whole volume as very amusing reading."—*Pall Mall Gazette*.

FIELD AND FOREST RAMBLES OF A NATURALIST IN NEW BRUNSWICK. With Notes and Observations on the Natural History of Eastern Canada. By **A. Leith Adams, M.A.**, &c., Author of "Wanderings of a Naturalist in India," &c., &c. In 8vo, cloth. Illustrated. 14s.

"Will be found interesting by those who take a pleasure either in sport or natural history."—*Athenæum*.
"The descriptions are clear and full of interest, while the book is prevented from degenerating into a mere scientific catalogue by many graphic sketches of the rambles."—*John Bull*.
"To the naturalist the book will be most valuable. . . . To the general reader the book will prove most interesting, for the style is pleasant and chatty, and the information given is so graphic and full, that those who care nothing for natural history as a pursuit will yet read these descriptions with great interest."—*Evening Standard*.
"Both sportsmen and naturalists will find this work replete with anecdote and carefully-recorded observation, which will entertain them."—*Nature*.

TENT LIFE WITH ENGLISH GIPSIES IN NORWAY. By **Hubert Smith**. In 8vo, cloth. Five full-page Engravings, and 31 smaller Illustrations, with Map of the Country showing Routes. Price 21s.

"If any of our readers think of scraping an acquaintance with Norway, let them read this book. The gypsies, always an interesting study, become doubly interesting, when we are, as in these pages, introduced to them in their daily walk and conversation."—*Examiner*.
"Written in a very lively style, and has throughout a smack of dry humour and satiric reflection which shows the writer to be a keen observer of men and things. We hope that many will read it and find in it the same amusement as ourselves."—*Times*.

65, Cornhill; & 12, Paternoster Row, London.

Works Published by Henry S. King & Co.,

VOYAGES AND TRAVEL—*continued.*

FAYOUM; OR, ARTISTS IN EGYPT. A Tour with M. Gérôme and others. By **J. Lenoir.** Crown 8vo, cloth. Illustrated. 7s. 6d.

"A pleasantly written and very readable book."—*Examiner.*

"The book is very amusing.... Who- ever may take it up will find he has with him a bright and pleasant companion."—*Spectator.*

SPITZBERGEN THE GATEWAY TO THE POLYNIA; OR, A VOYAGE TO SPITZBERGEN. By **Captain John C. Wells, R.N.** In 8vo, cloth. Profusely Illustrated. Price 21s.

"Straightforward and clear in style, securing our confidence by its unaffected simplicity and good sense."—*Saturday Review.*

"A charming book, remarkably well written and well illustrated."—*Standard.*

"Blends pleasantly science with adventure, picturesque sketches of a summer cruise among the wild sports and fantastic scenery of Spitzbergen, with earnest advocacy of Arctic Exploration."—*Graphic.*

AN AUTUMN TOUR IN THE UNITED STATES AND CANADA. By **Lieut.-Colonel Julius George Medley.** Crown 8vo. Price 5s.

"Colonel Medley's little volume is a pleasantly written account of a two-months' visit to America."—*Hour.*

"May be recommended as manly, sensible, and pleasantly written."—*Globe.*

THE NILE WITHOUT A DRAGOMAN. By **Frederic Eden.** Second Edition. In one vol. Crown 8vo, cloth. 7s. 6d.

"Should any of our readers care to imitate Mr. Eden's example, and wish to see things with their own eyes, and shift for themselves, next winter in Upper Egypt, they will find this book a very agreeable guide."—*Times.*

"It is a book to read during an autumn holiday."—*Spectator.*

"Gives, within moderate compass, a suggestive description of the charms, curiosities, dangers, and discomforts of the Nile voyage."—*Saturday Review.*

ROUND THE WORLD IN 1870. A Volume of Travels, with Maps. By **A. D. Carlisle, B.A.,** Trin. Coll., Camb. Demy 8vo. 16s.

"Makes one understand how going round the world is to be done in the quickest and pleasantest manner."—*Spectator.*

"We can only commend, which we do very heartily, an eminently sensible and readable book."—*British Quarterly Review.*

IRELAND IN 1872. A Tour of Observation, with Remarks on Irish Public Questions. By **Dr. James Macaulay.** Crown 8vo. 7s. 6d.

"A careful and instructive book. Full of facts, full of information, and full of interest."—*Literary Churchman.*

"We have rarely met a book on Ireland which for impartiality of criticism and general accuracy of information could be so well recommended to the fair-minded Irish reader."—*Evening Standard.*

"A deeply interesting account of what is called a tour of observation, and some noteworthy remarks on Irish public questions."—*Illustrated London News.*

OVER THE DOVREFJELDS. By **J. S. Shepard,** Author of "A Ramble through Norway," &c. Crown 8vo. Illustrated. Price 4s. 6d.

"We have read many books of Norwegian travel, but . . . we have seen none so pleasantly narrative in its style, and so varied in its subject."—*Spectator.*

"Is a well-timed book."—*Echo.*

"As interesting a little volume as could be written on the subject. So interesting and shortly written that it will commend itself to all intending tourists."—*Examiner.*

A WINTER IN MOROCCO. By **Amelia Perrier.** Large crown 8vo. Illustrated. Price 10s. 6d.

"Well worth reading, and contains several excellent illustrations."—*Hour.*

"Miss Perrier is a very amusing writer. She has a good deal of humour, sees the oddity and quaintness of Oriental life with a quick observant eye, and evidently turned her opportunities of sarcastic examination to account."—*Daily News.*

65, Cornhill; & 12, Paternoster Row, London.

SCIENCE.

PRINCIPLES OF MENTAL PHYSIOLOGY. With their Applications to the Training and Discipline of the Mind, and the Study of its Morbid Conditions. By **W. B. Carpenter, LL.D., M.D., F.R.S.**, &c. 8vo. Illustrated. *[Immediately.*

THE EXPANSE OF HEAVEN. A Series of Essays on the Wonders of the Firmament. By **R. A. Proctor, B.A.**, author of "Other Worlds," &c. Small Crown 8vo. *[Shortly.*

STUDIES OF BLAST FURNACE PHENOMENA. By **M. L. Gruner**, President of the General Council of Mines of France. Translated by **L. D. B. Gordon, F.R.S.E., F.G.S.**, &c. Demy 8vo. Price 7s. 6d.

These are some important practical studies by one of the most eminent metallurgical authorities of the Continent.

A LEGAL HANDBOOK FOR ARCHITECTS. By **Edward Jenkins** and **John Raymond, Esqrs.**, Barristers-at-Law. In 1 vol. Price 6s.

The Publishers are assured that this book will constitute an invaluable and necessary companion for every architect's and builder's table, as well as a useful introduction for architects' pupils to the practical law of their profession. Dedicated by special permission to the Royal Institution of British Architects.

CONTEMPORARY ENGLISH PSYCHOLOGY. From the French of Professor **Th. Ribot**. An Analysis of the Views and Opinions of the following Metaphysicians, as expressed in their writings:—

James Mill, A. Bain, John Stuart Mill, George H. Lewes, Herbert Spencer, Samuel Bailey. Large post 8vo.

PHYSIOLOGY FOR PRACTICAL USE. By various Eminent writers. Edited by **James Hinton**. 2 vols. Crown 8vo. With 50 illustrations.

These Papers have been prepared at great pains, and their endeavour is to familiarise the popular mind with those physiological truths which are needful to all who desire to keep the body in a state of health.

[In the Press.

THE PLACE OF THE PHYSICIAN. The Introductory Lecture at Guy's Hospital, 1873-4; to which is added
ESSAYS ON THE LAW OF HUMAN LIFE AND ON THE RELATION BETWEEN ORGANIC AND INORGANIC WORLDS.

By **James Hinton**, Author of "Man and His Dwelling-Place." Crown 8vo. Limp cloth.

SCIENCE—*continued*.

THE HISTORY OF THE NATURAL CREATION, Being a Series of Popular Scientific Lectures on the General Theory of Progression of Species; with a Dissertation on the Theories of Darwin and Goethe; more especially applying them to the Origin of Man, and to other Fundamental Questions of Natural Science connected therewith. By **Professor Ernst Hæckel**, of the University of Jena. 8vo. With Woodcuts and Plates.
[*In the Press.*

Second Edition.

CHANGE OF AIR AND SCENE. A Physician's Hints about Doctors, Patients, Hygiène, and Society; with Notes of Excursions for health in the Pyrenees, and amongst the Watering-places of France (Inland and Seaward), Switzerland, Corsica, and the Mediterranean. By **Dr. Alphonse Donné.** Large post 8vo. Price 9s.

"A very readable and serviceable book. . . . The real value of it is to be found in the accurate and minute information given with regard to a large number of places which have gained a reputation on the continent for their mineral waters."—*Pall Mall Gazette*.
"A singularly pleasant and chatty as well as instructive book about health."—*Guardian*.

MISS YOUMANS' FIRST BOOK OF BOTANY. Designed to cultivate the observing powers of Children. From the Author's latest Stereotyped Edition. New and Enlarged Edition, with 300 Engravings. Crown 8vo. 5s.

"It is but rarely that a school-book appears which is at once so novel in plan, so successful in execution, and so suited to the general want, as to command universal and unqualified approbation, but such has been the case with Miss Youmans' First Book of Botany. . . . It has been everywhere welcomed as a timely and invaluable contribution to the improvement of primary education."—*Pall Mall Gazette*.

AN ARABIC AND ENGLISH DICTIONARY OF THE KORAN. By **Major J. Penrice, B.A.** 4to. Price 21s.

MODERN GOTHIC ARCHITECTURE. By **T. G. Jackson.** Crown 8vo. Price 5s.

"The reader will find some of the most important doctrines of eminent art teachers practically applied in this little book, which is well written and popular in style."—*Manchester Examiner*.
"Much clearness, force, wealth of illustration, and in style of composition, which tends to commend his views."—*Edinburgh Daily Review*.
"This thoughtful little book is worthy of the perusal of all interested in art or architecture."—*Standard*.

A TREATISE ON RELAPSING FEVER. By **R. T. Lyons,** Assistant-Surgeon, Bengal Army. Small post 8vo. 7s. 6d.

"A practical work thoroughly supported in its views by a series of remarkable cases."—*Standard*.

SCIENCE—*continued*.

FOUR WORKS BY DR. EDWARD SMITH.

I. **HEALTH AND DISEASE**, as influenced by the Daily, Seasonal and other Cyclical Changes in the Human System. A New Edit. 7s. 6d.

II. **FOODS**. Second Edition. Profusely Illustrated. Price 5s.

III. **PRACTICAL DIETARY FOR FAMILIES, SCHOOLS, AND THE LABOURING CLASSES**. A New Edit. Price 3s. 6d.

IV. **CONSUMPTION IN ITS EARLY AND REMEDIABLE STAGES**. A New Edit. 7s. 6d.

THE PORT OF REFUGE; OR, COUNSEL AND AID TO SHIPMASTERS IN DIFFICULTY, DOUBT, OR DISTRESS. By **Manley Hopkins**, Author of "A Handbook of Average," "A Manual of Insurance," &c. Cr. 8vo. Price 6s.

SUBJECTS:—The Shipmaster's Position and Duties.—Agents and Agency.—Average.—Bottomry, and other Means of Raising Money.—The Charter-Party, and Bill-of-Lading. Stoppage in Transitu; and the Shipowner's Lien.—Collision.

"Combines in quite a marvellous manner a fullness of information which will make it perfectly indispensable in the captain's bookcase, and equally suitable to the gentleman's library. This synopsis of the law of shipping in all its multifarious ramifications and the hints he gives on a variety of topics must be invaluable to the master mariner whenever he is in doubt, difficulty, and danger."—*Mercantile Marine Magazine.*

"A truly excellent contribution to the literature of our marine commerce."—*Echo.*

"Those immediately concerned will find it well worth while to avail themselves of its teachings."—*Colburn's U.S. Magazine.*

LOMBARD STREET. A Description of the Money Market. By **Walter Bagehot**. Large crown 8vo. Third Edition. 7s. 6d.

"An acceptable addition to the literature of finance."—*Stock Exchange Review.*

"Mr. Bagehot touches incidentally a hundred points connected with his subject, and pours serene white light upon them all."—*Spectator.*

"Anybody who wishes to have a clear idea of the workings of what is called the Money Market should procure a little volume which Mr. Bagehot has just published, and he will there find the whole thing in a nut-shell ... The subject is one, it is almost needless to say, on which Mr. Bagehot writes with the authority of a man who combines practical experience with scientific study."—*Saturday Review.*

"Besides its main topic, the management of the reserve of the Bank of England, it is full of the most interesting economic history."—*Athenæum.*

CHOLERA: HOW TO AVOID AND TREAT IT. Popular and Practical Notes by **Henry Blanc, M.D.** Crown 8vo. 4s. 6d.

65, *Cornhill;* & 12, *Paternoster Row, London.*

SCIENCE—*continued*.

THE INTERNATIONAL SCIENTIFIC SERIES.

Although these Works are not specially designed for the instruction of beginners, still, as they are intended to address the *non-scientific public*, they are, as far as possible, explanatory in character, and free from technicalities; the object of each author being to bring his subject as near as he can to the general reader.

The Volumes already Published are:—

Third Edition.

THE FORMS OF WATER IN RAIN AND RIVERS, ICE AND GLACIERS. By **J. Tyndall, LL.D., F.R.S.** With 26 Illustrations. Crown 8vo. 5*s*.

"One of Professor Tyndall's best scientific treatises."—*Standard*.
"With the clearness and brilliancy of language which have won for him his fame, he considers the subject of ice, snow, and glaciers."—*Morning Post*.

"Before starting for Switzerland next summer every one should study 'The forms of water.'"—*Globe*.
"Eloquent and instructive in an eminent degree."—*British Quarterly*.

Second Edition.

PHYSICS AND POLITICS; or, Thoughts on the Application of the Principles of "Natural Selection" and "Inheritance" to Political Society. By **Walter Bagehot.** Crown 8vo. 4*s*.

"On the whole we can recommend the book as well deserving to be read by thoughtful students of politics."—*Saturday Review*.

"Able and ingenious."—*Spectator*.
"A work of really original and interesting speculation."—*Guardian*.

Second Edition.

FOODS. By **Dr. Edward Smith.** Profusely Illustrated. Price 5*s*.

"A comprehensive résumé of our present chemical and physiological knowledge of the various foods, solid and liquid, which go so far to ameliorate the troubles and vexations of this anxious and wearying existence."—*Chemist and Druggist*.

"Heads of households will find it considerably to their advantage to study its contents."—*Court Express*.
"A very comprehensive book. Every page teems with information. Readable throughout."—*Church Herald*.

Second Edition.

MIND AND BODY; The Theories of their Relations. By **Alexander Bain, LL.D.**, Professor of Logic at the University of Aberdeen. Four Illustrations. 4*s*.

THE STUDY OF SOCIOLOGY. By **Herbert Spencer.** Crown 8vo. Price 5*s*.

ON THE CONSERVATION OF ENERGY. By **Professor Balfour Stewart.** Fourteen Engravings. Price 5*s*.

ANIMAL MECHANICS; or, Walking, Swimming, and Flying. By **Dr. J. B. Pettigrew, M.D., F.R.S.**

65, *Cornhill; & 12, Paternoster Row, London.*

LIST OF AUTHORS AND SUBJECTS OF THEIR BOOKS,

TO BE PUBLISHED IN THE

INTERNATIONAL SCIENTIFIC SERIES.

Dr. HENRY MAUDSLEY.
: Responsibility in Mental Disease.

Prof. E. J. MAREY.
: The Animal Frame.

Rev. M. J. BERKELEY, M.A., F.L.S., and M. COOKE, M.A., LL.D.
: Fungi; their Nature, Influences, and Uses.

Prof. OSCAR SCHMIDT, (University of Strasburg).
: The Theory of Descent and Darwinism.

Prof. W. KINGDOM CLIFFORD, M.A.
: The First Principles of the Exact Sciences explained to the non-mathematical.

Prof. T. H. HUXLEY, LL.D., F.R.S.
: Bodily Motion and Consciousness.

Dr. W. B. CARPENTER, LL.D., F.R.S.
: The Physical Geography of the Sea.

Prof. WILLIAM ODLING, F.R.S.
: The New Chemistry.

Prof. SHELDON AMOS.
: The Science of Law.

W. LAUDER LINDSAY, M.D., F.R.S.E.
: Mind in the Lower Animals.

Sir JOHN LUBBOCK, Bart., F.R.S.
: The Antiquity of Man.

Prof. W. T. THISELTON DYER, B.A., B.SC.
: Form and Habit in Flowering Plants.

Mr. J. N. LOCKYER, F.R.S.
: Spectrum Analysis.

Prof. MICHAEL FOSTER, M.D.
: Protoplasm and the Cell Theory.

Prof. W. STANLEY JEVONS.
: The Logic of Statistics.

Dr. H. CHARLTON BASTIAN, M.D., F.R.S.
: The Brain as an Organ of Mind.

Prof. A. C. RAMSAY, LL.D., F.R.S.
: Earth Sculpture: Hills, Valleys, Mountains, Plains, Rivers, Lakes; how they were Produced, and how they have been Destroyed.

Prof. RUDOLPH VIRCHOW, (University of Berlin).
: Morbid Physiological Action.

Prof. CLAUDE BERNARD.
: Physical and Metaphysical Phenomena of Life.

Prof. A. QUETELET.
: Social Physics.

Prof. H. SAINTE-CLAIRE DEVILLE.
: An Introduction to General Chemistry.

Prof. WURTZ.
: Atoms and the Atomic Theory.

Prof. DE QUATREFAGES.
: The Negro Races.

Prof. LACAZE-DUTHIERS.
: Zoology since Cuvier.

Prof. BERTHELOT.
: Chemical Synthesis.

Prof. J. ROSENTHAL.
: General Physiology of Muscles and Nerves.

Prof. JAMES D. DANA, M.A., LL.D.
: On Cephalization; or, Head-Characters in the Gradation and Progress of Life.

Prof. S. W. JOHNSON, M.A.
: On the Nutrition of Plants.

Prof. AUSTIN FLINT, Jr. M.D.
: The Nervous System and its Relation to the Bodily Functions.

Prof. W. D. WHITNEY.
: Modern Linguistic Science.

Prof. BERNSTEIN (University of Halle).
: Physiology of the Senses.

Prof. FERDINAND COHN, (University of Breslau).
: Thallophytes (Algae, Lichens, Fungi).

Prof. HERMANN (University of Zurich).
: Respiration.

Prof. LEUCKART (University of Leipsic).
: Outlines of Animal Organization.

Prof. LIEBREICH (University of Berlin).
: Outlines of Toxicology.

Prof. KUNDT (University of Strasburg).
: On Sound.

Prof. LOMMEL (University of Erlangen).
: Optics.

Prof. REES (University of Erlangen).
: On Parasitic Plants.

Prof. STEINTHAL (University of Berlin).
: Outlines of the Science of Language.

Prof. VOGEL (Polytechnic Acad. of Berlin).
: The Chemical Effects of Light.

ESSAYS, LECTURES, AND COLLECTED PAPERS.

IN STRANGE COMPANY; or, The Note Book of a Roving Correspondent. By James Greenwood, "The Amateur Casual." Crown 8vo. 6s.

MASTER-SPIRITS. By Robert Buchanan. Post 8vo. 10s. 6d.

"Good Books are the precious life-blood of Master-Spirits."—*Milton.*

Criticism as a Fine Art.
Charles Dickens.
Tennyson.
Browning's Martsyneco.
A Young English Positivist.
Hugo in 1872.
Prose and Verse.

Birds of the Hebrides.
Scandinavian Studies:—
1. A Morning in Copenhagen.
2. Bjornsen's Masterpiece.
3. Old Ballads of Denmark.

4. Modern Danish Ballads.
Poets in Obscurity:—
1. George Heath, the Moorland Poet.
2. William Miller.

These are some of the author's lighter and more generally interesting Essays on literary topics of permanent interest. His other prose contributions, critical and philosophical, to our literature are included in the collected editions of his works.

THEOLOGY IN THE ENGLISH POETS. Being Lectures delivered by the Rev. Stopford A. Brooke, Chaplain in Ordinary to Her Majesty the Queen.

MOUNTAIN, MEADOW, AND MERE; a Series of Outdoor Sketches of Sport, Scenery, Adventures, and Natural History. By G. Christopher Davies. With 16 Illustrations by W. Harcourt. Crown 8vo, price 6s.

HOW TO AMUSE AND EMPLOY OUR INVALIDS. By Harriet Power. Fcap. 8vo. Price 2s. 6d.

What Invalids may do to Amuse Themselves.
What Friends and Attendants may do for them.
Articles for comfort in a Sick Room.

Amusement for Invalid Children.
To the Invalid.
Comforts and Employment for the Aged.
Employment for Sunday.

The question, so often put by invalids, "Can you not find me something to do?" is answered at some length in this little book, which takes up a subject but little touched upon in the many manuals for nurses. [*Just out.*

STUDIES AND ROMANCES. By H. Schutz Wilson. 1 vol. Crown 8vo. Price 7s. 6d.

Shakespeare in Blackfriars.
The Loves of Goethe.
Romance of the Thames.
An Exalted Hora.
Two Sprigs of Edelweiss.
Between Moor and Main.
An Episode of the Terror.

Harry Ormond's Christmas Dinner.
Agnes Bernauerin.
"Yes" or "No"?
A Model Romance.
The Story of Little Jenny.
Dining.
The Record of a Vanished Life.

"Vivacious and interesting."—*Scotsman.*
"Open the book, however, at what page the reader may, he will find something to amuse and instruct, and he must be very hard to please if he finds nothing to suit him, either grave or gay, stirring or romantic, in the capital stories collected in this well-got-up volume."—*John Bull.*

Works Published by Henry S. King & Co., 13

ESSAYS, LECTURES, ETC.—*continued.*

SHORT LECTURES ON THE LAND LAWS. Delivered before the Working Men's College. By **T. Leman Wilkinson.** Crown 8vo, limp cloth. 2s.

"A very handy and intelligible epitome of the general principles of existing land laws."—*Standard.*

"A very clear and lucid statement as to the condition of the present land laws which govern our country. These Lectures possess the advantage of not being loaded with superfluous matter."—*Civil Service Gazette.*

AN ESSAY ON THE CULTURE OF THE OBSERVING POWERS OF CHILDREN, especially in connection with the Study of Botany. By **Eliza A. Youmans.** Edited, with Notes and a Supplement, by **Joseph Payne,** F.C.P., Author of "Lectures on the Science and Art of Education," &c. Crown 8vo. 2s. 6d.

"This study, according to her just notions on the subject, is to be fundamentally based on the exercise of the pupil's own powers of observation. He is to see and examine the properties of plants and flowers at first hand, not merely to be informed of what others have seen and examined."—*Pall Mall Gazette.*

THE GENIUS OF CHRISTIANITY UNVEILED. Being Essays by **William Godwin,** Author of "Political Justice," &c. Never before published. 1 vol., crown 8vo. 7s. 6d.

"Few have thought more clearly and directly than William Godwin, or expressed their reflections with more simplicity and nerveness."—*Examiner.*

"The deliberate thoughts of Godwin deserve to be put before the world for reading and consideration."—*Athenæum.*

THE PELICAN PAPERS. Reminiscences and Remains of a Dweller in the Wilderness. By **James Ashcroft Noble.** Crown 8vo. 6s.

"Written somewhat after the fashion of Mr. Helps's 'Friends in Council.'"—*Examiner.*

"Will well repay perusal by all thoughtful and intelligent readers."—*Liverpool Leader.*

"The 'Pelican Papers' make a very readable volume."—*Civilian.*

BRIEFS AND PAPERS. Being Sketches of the Bar and the Press. By **Two Idle Apprentices.** Crown 8vo. 7s. 6d.

"Written with spirit and knowledge, and give some curious glimpses into what the majority will regard as strange and unknown territories."—*Daily News.*

"This is one of the best books to while away an hour and cause a generous laugh that we have come across for a long time."—*John Bull.*

65, *Cornhill; & 12, Paternoster Row, London.*

ESSAYS, LECTURES, ETC.—*continued.*

THE SECRET OF LONG LIFE. Dedicated by Special Permission to Lord St. Leonards. Third Edition. Large crown 8vo. 5s.

"A charming little volume."—*Times.*
"A very pleasant little book, cheerful, genial, scholarly."—*Spectator.*
"We should recommend our readers to get this book."—*British Quarterly Review.*
"Entitled to the warmest admiration."—*Pall Mall Gazette.*

SOLDIERING AND SCRIBBLING. By Archibald Forbes, of the *Daily News*, Author of "My Experience of the War between France and Germany." Crown 8vo. 7s. 6d.

"All who open it will be inclined to read through for the varied entertainment which it affords."—*Daily News.*
"There is a good deal of instruction to outsiders touching military life, in this volume."—*Evening Standard.*
"Thoroughly readable and worth reading."—*Scotsman.*

THE ENGLISH CONSTITUTION. By Walter Bagehot. A New Edition, revised and corrected, with an Introductory Dissertation on recent changes and events. Crown 8vo. 7s. 6d.

"A pleasing and clever study on the department of higher politics."—*Guardian.*
"No writer before him had set out so clearly what the efficient part of the English Constitution really is."—*Pall Mall Gazette.*
"Clear and practical."—*Globe.*

REPUBLICAN SUPERSTITIONS. Illustrated by the Political History of the United States. Including a Correspondence with M. Louis Blanc. By Moncure D. Conway. Crown 8vo. 5s.

"A very able exposure of the most plausible fallacies of Republicanism, by a writer of remarkable vigour and purity of style."—*Standard.*
"Mr. Conway writes with ardent sincerity. He gives us some good anecdotes, and he is occasionally almost eloquent."—*Guardian,* July 2, 1873.

STREAMS FROM HIDDEN SOURCES. By B. Montgomerie Ranking. Crown 8vo. 6s.

"In point of style it is well executed, and the prefatory notices are very good."—*Spectator.*
"The effect of reading the seven tales he presents to us is to make us wish for some seven more of the same kind."—*Pall Mall Gazette.*
"The tales are given throughout in the quaint version of the earliest English translators, and in the introduction to each will be found much curious information as to their origin, and the fate which they have met at the hands of later transcribers or imitators, and much tasteful appreciation of the varied sources from whence they are extracted. . . . We doubt not that Mr. Ranking's enthusiasm will communicate itself to many of his readers, and induce them in like manner to follow back these streamlets to their parent river."—*Graphic.*

MILITARY WORKS.

THE GERMAN ARTILLERY IN THE BATTLES NEAR METZ. Based on the official reports of the German Artillery. By **Captain Hoffbauer**, Instructor in the German Artillery and Engineer School. Translated by **Capt. E. O. Hollist.**

This history gives a detailed account of the movements of the German artillery in the three days' fighting to the east and west of Metz, which resulted in paralyzing the army under Marshal Bazaine, and its subsequent surrender. The action of the batteries with reference to the other arms is clearly explained, and the valuable maps show the positions taken up by the individual batteries at each stage of the contests. Tables are also supplied in the Appendix, furnishing full details as to the number of killed and wounded, expenditure of ammunition, &c. The campaign of 1870—71 having demonstrated the importance of artillery to an extent which has not previously been conceded to it, this work forms a valuable part of the literature of the campaign, and will be read with interest not only by members of the regular but also by those of the auxiliary forces.

THE OPERATIONS OF THE FIRST ARMY, UNDER STEINMETZ. By **Von Schell.** Translated by **Captain E. O. Hollist.** Demy 8vo. Uniform with the other volumes in the Series. Price 10s. 6d.

THE OPERATIONS OF THE BAVARIAN ARMY CORPS. By **Captain Hugo Helvig.** Translated by **Captain G. S. Schwabe.** With 5 large Maps. Demy 8vo. Uniform with the other Books in the Series.

DRILL REGULATIONS OF THE AUSTRIAN CAVALRY. From an Abridged Edition compiled by CAPTAIN ILLIA WOERNOVITS, of the General Staff, on the Tactical Regulations of the Austrian Army, and prefaced by a General Sketch of the Organisation, &c., of the Country. Translated by **Captain W. S. Cooke.** Crown 8vo, limp cloth.

THE OPERATIONS OF THE FIRST ARMY UNDER GEN. VON GOEBEN. By **Major Von Schell.** Translated by **Col. C. H. Von Wright.** Four Maps. Demy 8vo. 9s.

History of the Organisation, Equipment, and War Services of

THE REGIMENT OF BENGAL ARTILLERY. Compiled from Published Official and other Records, and various private sources, by **Major Francis W. Stubbs,** Royal (late Bengal) Artillery. Vol. I. will contain WAR SERVICES. The Second Volume will be published separately, and will contain the HISTORY OF THE ORGANISATION AND EQUIPMENT OF THE REGIMENT. In 2 vols. 8vo. With Maps and Plans. [*Preparing.*

MILITARY WORKS—*continued.*

THE ABOLITION OF PURCHASE AND THE ARMY REGULATION BILL OF 1871. By Lieut.-Col. the Hon. A. Anson, V.C., M.P. Crown 8vo. Price One Shilling.

THE STORY OF THE SUPERSESSIONS. By Lieut.-Col. the Hon. A. Anson, V.C., M.P. Crown 8vo. Price Sixpence.

ARMY RESERVES AND MILITIA REFORMS. By Lieut.-Col. the Hon. A. Anson. Crown 8vo. Sewed. Price One Shilling.

VICTORIES AND DEFEATS. An Attempt to explain the Causes which have led to them. An Officer's Manual. By Col. R. P. Anderson. Demy 8vo. 14s.

"A delightful military classic, and what is more, a most useful one. The young officer should have it always at hand to open anywhere and read a bit, and we warrant him that let that bit be ever so small it will give him material for an hour's thinking."—*United Service Gazette.*

THE FRONTAL ATTACK OF INFANTRY: By Capt. Laymann, Instructor of Tactics at the Military College, Neisse. Translated by Colonel Edward Newdigate. Crown 8vo, limp cloth. Price 2s. 6d.

"This work has met with special attention in our army."—*Militarin Wochenblatt.*

THE OPERATIONS OF THE FIRST ARMY IN NORTHERN FRANCE AGAINST FAIDHERBE. By Colonel Count Hermann Von Wartensleben, Chief of the Staff of the First Army. Translated by Colonel C. H. Von Wright. In demy 8vo. Uniform with the above. Price 9s.

"Very clear, simple, yet eminently instructive, is this history. It is not overladen with useless details, is written in good taste, and possesses the inestimable value of being in great measure the record of operations actually witnessed by the author, supplemented by official documents."—*Athenæum.*

"The work is based on the official war documents—it is especially valuable—the narrative is remarkably vivid and interesting. Two well-executed maps enable the reader to trace out the scenes of General Manteuffel's operations."—*Naval and Military Gazette.*

ELEMENTARY MILITARY GEOGRAPHY, RECONNOITRING, AND SKETCHING. Compiled for Non-Commissioned Officers and Soldiers of all Arms. By Lieut. C. E. H. Vincent, Royal Welsh Fusileers. Small crown 8vo. 2s. 6d.

"An admirable little manual full of facts and teachings."—*United Service Gazette.*

65, Cornhill; & 12, Paternoster Row, London.

MILITARY WORKS—*continued.*

STUDIES IN THE NEW INFANTRY TACTICS. Parts I. & II. By **Major W. Von Schereff.** Translated from the German by Col. **Lumley Graham.** Price 7s. 6d.

"Major Von Schereff's 'Studies in Tactics' is worthy of the perusal—indeed, of the thoughtful study—of every military man. The subject of the respective advantages of attack and defence, and of the methods in which each form of battle should be carried out under the fire of modern arms, is exhaustively and admirably treated; indeed, we cannot but consider it to be decidedly superior to any work which has hitherto appeared in English upon this all-important subject."—*Standard.*

TACTICAL DEDUCTIONS FROM THE WAR OF 1870—1. By **Captain A. Von Boguslawski.** Translated by **Colonel Lumley Graham**, late 18th (Royal Irish) Regiment. Demy 8vo. Uniform with the above. Price 7s.

"Major Boguslawski's tactical deductions from the war are, that infantry still preserve their superiority over cavalry, that open order must henceforth be the main principles of all drill, and that the chassepot is the best of all small arms for precision. . . . We must, without delay, impress brain and forethought into the British Service; and we cannot commence the good work too soon, or better, than by placing the two books ('The Operations of the German Armies' and 'Tactical Deductions') we have here criticised, in every military library, and introducing them as class-books in every tactical school."—*United Service Gazette.*

THE ARMY OF THE NORTH-GERMAN CONFEDERATION. A Brief Description of its Organisation, of the different Branches of the Service and their 'Rôle' in War, of its Mode of Fighting, &c. By a **Prussian General.** Translated from the German by Col. **Edward Newdigate.** Demy 8vo. 5s.

*** The authorship of this book was erroneously ascribed to the renowned General von Moltke, but there can be little doubt that it was written under his immediate inspiration.

THE OPERATIONS OF THE GERMAN ARMIES IN FRANCE, FROM SEDAN TO THE END OF THE WAR OF 1870—1. With Large Official Map. From the Journals of the Head-quarters Staff, by **Major Wm. Blume.** Translated by **E. M. Jones**, Major 20th Foot, late Professor of Military History, Sandhurst. Demy 8vo. Price 9s.

"The book is of absolute necessity to the military student. . . . The work is one of high merit."—*United Service Gazette.*
"The work of translation has been well done. In notes, prefaces, and introductions, much additional information has been given."—*Athenæum.*
"The work of Major von Blume in its English dress forms the most valuable addition to our stock of works upon the war that our press has put forth. Major Blume writes with a clear conciseness much wanting in many of his country's historians. Our space forbids our doing more than commending it earnestly as the most authentic and instructive narrative of the second section of the war that has yet appeared."—*Saturday Review.*

THE OPERATIONS OF THE SOUTH ARMY IN JANUARY AND FEBRUARY, 1871. Compiled from the Official War Documents of the Head-quarters of the Southern Army. By **Count Hermann Von Wartensleben**, Colonel in the Prussian General Staff. Translated by **Colonel C. H. Von Wright.** Demy 8vo, with Maps. Uniform with the above. Price 6s.

MILITARY WORKS—*continued.*

HASTY INTRENCHMENTS. By Colonel **A. Brialmont.** Translated by **Lieutenant Charles A. Empson, B.A.** Demy 8vo. Nine Plates. Price 6s.

"A valuable contribution to military literature."—*Athenæum.*

"In seven short chapters it gives plain directions for forming shelter-trenches, with the best method of carrying the necessary tools, and it offers practical illustrations of the use of hasty intrenchments on the field of battle."—*United Service Magazine.*

"It supplies that which our own text-books give but imperfectly, viz., hints as to how a position can best be strengthened by means ... of such extemporised intrenchments and batteries as can be thrown up by infantry in the space of four or five hours ... deserves to become a standard military work."—*Standard.*

"Clearly and critically written."—*Wellington Gazette.*

STUDIES IN LEADING TROOPS. By Colonel **Von Verdy Du Vernois.** An authorised and accurate Translation by **Lieutenant H. J. T. Hildyard,** 71st Foot. Parts I. and II. Demy 8vo. Price 7s.

*** General BEAUCHAMP WALKER says of this work:—"I recommend the first two numbers of Colonel von Verdy's 'Studies' to the attentive perusal of my brother officers. They supply a want which I have often felt during my service in this country, namely, a minuter tactical detail of the minor operations of the war than any but the most observant and fortunately-placed staff-officer is in a position to give. I have read and re-read them very carefully, I hope with profit, certainly with great interest, and believe that practice, in the sense of these 'Studies,' would be a valuable preparation for manœuvres on a more extended scale."—Berlin, June, 1872.

THE SUBSTANTIVE SENIORITY ARMY LIST, Majors and Captains. By **Captain F. B. P. White,** 1st W. I. Regiment. 8vo, sewed. 2s. 6d.

CAVALRY FIELD DUTY. By **Major-General Von Mirus.** Translated by **Captain Frank S. Russell,** 14th (King's) Hussars. Crown 8vo, limp cloth. 7s. 6d.

*** This is the text-book of instruction in the German cavalry, and comprises all the details connected with the military duties of cavalry soldiers on service. The translation is made from a new edition, which contains the modifications introduced consequent on the experiences of the late war. The great interest that students feel in all the German military methods, will, it is believed, render this book especially acceptable at the present time.

DISCIPLINE AND DRILL. Four Lectures delivered to the London Scottish Rifle Volunteers. By **Captain S. Flood Page.** A New and Cheaper Edition. Price 1s.

"One of the best-known and coolest-headed of the metropolitan regiments, whose adjutant moreover has lately published an admirable collection of lectures addressed by him to the men of his corps."—*Times.*

"The very useful and interesting work."—*Volunteer Service Gazette.*

INDIA AND THE EAST.

THE ORIENTAL SPORTING MAGAZINE. A Reprint of the first 5 Volumes, in 2 Volumes, demy 8vo. price 28s.

These volumes contain many quaint and clever papers, among which we may mention the famous Sporting Songs written by S. Y. S., of "The Boar, Saddle, Spur, and Spear," &c., &c.—Capt. Morris, of the Bombay Army; as well as descriptions of Hog Hunts, Fox Hunts, Lion Hunts, Tiger Hunts, and Cheeta Hunts; accounts of Shooting Excursions for Snipe, Partridges, Quail, Toucan, Ortolan, and Wild Fowl; interesting details of Pigeon Matches, Cock Fights, Horse, Tattoo, and Donkey Races: descriptions of the Origin, Regulations, and Uniforms of Hunting Clubs; Natural History of rare Wild Animals; Memoranda of Feats of Noted Horses; and Memoirs and Anecdotes of celebrated Sporting characters, &c., &c.
[*Just out.*

THE EUROPEAN IN INDIA. A Hand-book of Practical Information for those proceeding to, or residing in, the East Indies, relating to Outfits, Routes, Time for Departure, Indian Climate, &c. By **Edmund C. P. Hull.** With a MEDICAL GUIDE FOR ANGLO-INDIANS. Being a Compendium of Advice to Europeans in India, relating to the Preservation and Regulation of Health. By **R. S. Mair, M.D., F.R.C.S.E.**, Late Deputy Coroner of Madras. In 1 vol. Post 8vo. 6s.

"Full of all sorts of useful information to the English settler or traveller in India."—*Standard.*
"One of the most valuable books ever published in India—valuable for its sound information, its careful array of pertinent facts, and its sterling common sense. It is a publisher's as well as an author's 'hit,' for it supplies a want which few persons may have discovered, but which everybody will at once recognise when once the contents of the book have been mastered. The medical part of the work is invaluable."—*Calcutta Guardian.*

THE MEDICAL GUIDE FOR ANGLO-INDIANS. Being a Compendium of advice to Europeans in India, relating to the Preservation and Regulation of Health. By **R. S. Mair, F.R.C.S.E.**, late Deputy Coroner of Madras. Reprinted, with numerous additions and corrections, from "The European in India."

EASTERN EXPERIENCES. By **L. Bowring, C.S.I.**, Lord Canning's Private Secretary, and for many years the Chief Commissioner of Mysore and Coorg. In 1 vol. Demy 8vo. 16s. Illustrated with Maps and Diagrams.

"An admirable and exhaustive geographical, political, and industrial survey."—*Athenæum.*
"The usefulness of this compact and methodical summary of the most authentic information relating to countries whose welfare is intimately connected with our own, should obtain for Mr. Lewin Bowring's work a good place among treatises of its kind."—*Daily News.*
"Interesting even to the general reader, but more especially so to those who may have a special concern in that portion of our Indian Empire."—*Post.*

TAS-HĪL UL KALĀM; OR, HINDUSTANI MADE EASY. By **Captain W. R. M. Holroyd,** Bengal Staff Corps, Director of Public Instruction, Punjab. Crown 8vo. Price 5s.

65, *Cornhill;* & 12, *Paternoster Row, London.*

INDIA AND THE EAST—*continued.*

WESTERN INDIA BEFORE AND DURING THE MUTINIES. Pictures drawn from Life. By **Major-Gen. Sir George Le Grand Jacob, K.C.S.I., C.B.** In 1 vol. Crown 8vo. 7s. 6d.

"The most important contribution to the history of Western India during the Mutinies which has yet, in a popular form been made public."—*Athenæum.*

"Few men more competent than himself to speak authoritatively concerning Indian affairs."—*Standard.*

EDUCATIONAL COURSE OF SECULAR SCHOOL BOOKS FOR INDIA. Edited by **J. S. Laurie**, of the Inner Temple, Barrister-at-Law; formerly H.M. Inspector of Schools, England; Assistant Royal Commissioner, Ireland; Special Commissioner, African Settlements; Director of Public Instruction, Ceylon.

EXTRACT FROM PROSPECTUS.

The Editor has undertaken to frame for India,—what he has been eminently successful in doing for England and her colonies,—a series of educational works, which he hopes will prove as suitable for the peculiar wants of the country as they will be consistent with the leading idea above alluded to. Like all beginnings, his present instalments are necessarily somewhat meagre and elementary; but he only awaits official and public approval to complete, within a comparatively brief period, his contemplated plan of a specific and fairly comprehensive series of works in the various leading vernaculars of the Indian continent. Meanwhile, those on his general catalogue may be found suitable, in their present form, for use in the Anglo-vernacular and English schools of India.

The following Works are now ready:—

	s. d.		s. d.
THE FIRST HINDUSTANI READER, stiff linen wrapper	0 6	GEOGRAPHY OF INDIA, with Maps and Historical Appendix, tracing the growth of the British Empire in Hindustan. 128 pp. Cloth	1 6
Ditto ditto strongly bound in cloth	0 9		
THE SECOND HINDUSTANI READER, stiff linen wrapper	0 6		
Ditto ditto strongly bound in cloth	0 9		

In the Press.

ELEMENTARY GEOGRAPHY OF INDIA.

FACTS AND FEATURES OF INDIAN HISTORY, in a series of alternating Reading Lessons and Memory Exercises.

EXCHANGE TABLES OF STERLING AND INDIAN RUPEE CURRENCY, UPON A NEW AND EXTENDED SYSTEM, embracing Values from One Farthing to One Hundred Thousand Pounds, and at rates progressing, in Sixteenths of a Penny, from 1s. 9d. to 2s. 3d. per Rupee. By **Donald Fraser,** Accountant to the British Indian Steam Navigation Co., Limited. Royal 8vo. 10s. 6d.

"The calculations must have entailed great labour on the author, but the work is one which we fancy must become a standard one in all business houses which have dealings with any country where the rupee and the English pound are standard coins of currency."—*Inverness Courier.*

65, *Cornhill;* & 12, *Paternoster Row, London.*

Works Published by Henry S. King & Co.,

BOOKS FOR THE YOUNG AND FOR LENDING LIBRARIES.

LAYS OF MANY LANDS. By a **Knight Errant.** Illustrated. Crown 8vo.
  Pharaoh Land.   Wonder Land.
  Home Land.   Rhine Land.

SEEKING HIS FORTUNE, AND OTHER STORIES. Crown 8vo. Four Illustrations. Price 3s. 6d.
 Contents.—Seeking his Fortune.—Oluf and Stephanoff.—What's in a Name?—Contrast.—Onesta.
 A series of instructive and interesting stories for children of both sexes, each one enforcing, indirectly, a good moral lesson.

DADDY'S PET. By **Mrs. Ellen Ross (Nelsie Brook).** Square crown 8vo, uniform with "Lost Gip." 6 Illustrations.
 A pathetic story of lowly life, showing the good influence of home and of child-life upon an uncultivated but true-hearted "navvy."

THREE WORKS BY MARTHA FARQUHARSON.
Each Story is independent and complete in itself. They are published in uniform size and price, and are elegantly bound and illustrated.

I. **ELSIE DINSMORE.** Crown 8vo. 3s. 6d.

II. **ELSIE'S GIRLHOOD.** Crown 8vo. 3s. 6d.

III. **ELSIE'S HOLIDAYS AT ROSELANDS.** Crown 8vo. 3s. 6d.
 The Stories by this author have a very high reputation in America, and of all her books these are the most popular and widely circulated. These are the only English editions sanctioned by the author, who has a direct interest in this English Edition.

LOST GIP. By **Hesba Stretton,** Author of "Little Meg," "Alone in London." Square crown 8vo. Six Illustrations. Price 1s. 6d.
 *** *A HANDSOMELY BOUND EDITION, WITH TWELVE ILLUSTRATIONS, PRICE HALF-A-CROWN.*
 "Thoroughly enlists the sympathies of the reader."—*Church Review.* *formit.*
 "Full of tender touches."—*Nonconf.* "An exquisitely touching little story."—*Church Herald.*

THE KING'S SERVANTS. By **Hesba Stretton,** Author of "Lost Gip." Square crown 8vo, uniform with "Lost Gip." 8 Illustrations. Price 1s. 6d.
 Part I.—Faithful in Little. Part II.—Unfaithful. Part III.—Faithful in Much.

AT SCHOOL WITH AN OLD DRAGOON. By **Stephen J. Mac Kenna.** Crown 8vo. 5s. With Six Illustrations.
 "At Ghuznee Villa." In a Golden Fort. A Baptism of Frost.
 Introductory.   A Little Game.   Who Shot the Kafirs.
 Henry and Amy.   True to his Salt.   John Chinaman and the
 A Story of Canterbury. Mother Moran's Enemies. Middies.
 A Disastrous Trumpet Call. Sooka the Syce; or, Sea
 A Baptism of Fire.   Horses in Reality.
 A Series of Stories of Military and Naval Adventure, related by an old Retired Officer of the Army.

65, Cornhill; & 12, Paternoster Row, London.

BOOKS FOR THE YOUNG, ETC.—*continued.*

FANTASTIC STORIES. Translated from the German of **Richard Leander**, by **Paulina B. Granville**. Crown 8vo. Eight full-page Illustrations.

- The Magic Organ.
- The Invisible Kingdom.
- The Knight who Grew Rusty.
- Of the Queen who could not make Gingerbread Nuts, and of the King who could not play the Jew's Harp.
- The Wishing Ring.
- The Three Princesses with Hearts of Glass.
- The Old Bachelor.
- Sepp's Courtship.
- Heino in the Marsh.
- Unlucky Dog and Fortune's Favourite.
- The Dreaming Beech.
- The Little Hump-Backed Maiden.
- Heavenly Music.
- The Old Hair Trunk.

These are translations of some of the best of Richard Leander's well-known stories for children. The illustrations to this work are of singular beauty and finish.

THE AFRICAN CRUISER. A Midshipman's Adventures on the West Coast. A Book for Boys. By **S. Whitchurch Sadler, R.N.** Three Illustrations. Crown 8vo. 3s. 6d.

A book of real adventures among slavers on the West Coast of Africa. One chief recommendation is the faithfulness of the local colouring.

THE LITTLE WONDER-HORN. By **Jean Ingelow**. A Second Series of "*Stories told to a Child*." Fifteen Illustrations. Cloth, gilt. 3s. 6d.

"Full of fresh and vigorous fancy: it is worthy of the author of some of the best of our modern verse."—*Standard.*

"We like all the contents of the 'Little Wonder-Horn' very much."—*Athenæum.*
"We recommend it with confidence."—*Pall Mall Gazette.*

Second Edition.

BRAVE MEN'S FOOTSTEPS. A Book of Example and Anecdote for Young People. By the Editor of "**Men who have Risen.**" With Four Illustrations. By **C. Doyle**. 3s. 6d.

"The little volume is precisely of the stamp to win the favour of those who, in choosing a gift for a boy, would consult his moral development as well as his temporary pleasure."—*Daily Telegraph.*

"A readable and instructive volume."—*Examiner.*
"No more welcome book for the school-boy could be imagined."—*Birmingham Daily Gazette.*

Third Edition.

STORIES IN PRECIOUS STONES. By **Helen Zimmern**. With Six Illustrations. Crown 8vo. 5s.

"A pretty little book which fanciful young persons will appreciate, and which will remind its readers of many a legend, and many an imaginary virtue attached to the gems they are so fond of wearing."—*Post.*

"A series of pretty tales which are half fantastic, half natural, and pleasantly quaint, as befits stories intended for the young."—*Daily Telegraph.*

Second Edition.

GUTTA-PERCHA WILLIE, THE WORKING GENIUS, By **George Macdonald**. With Illustrations by **Arthur Hughes**. Crown 8vo. 3s. 6d.

"An amusing and instructive book."—*Yorkshire Post.*
"One of those charming books for which the author is so well known."—*Edinburgh Daily Review.*

"The cleverest child we know assures us she has read this story through five times. Mr. Macdonald will, we are convinced, accept that verdict upon his little work as final."—*Spectator.*

Works Published by Henry S. King & Co., 23

BOOKS FOR THE YOUNG, ETC.—*continued.*

THE TRAVELLING MENAGERIE. By **Charles Camden**, Author of "Hoity Toity." Illustrated by **J. Mahoney**. Crown 8vo. 3s. 6d.

"A capital little book .... deserves a wide circulation among our boys and girls."—*Hour.*

"A very attractive story."—*Public Opinion.*

PLUCKY FELLOWS. A Book for Boys. By **Stephen J. Mac Kenna.** With Six Illustrations. Crown 8vo. Price 3s. 6d.

"This is one of the very best 'Books for Boys' which have been issued this year."—*Morning Advertiser.*
"A thorough book for boys ... written

throughout in a manly straightforward manner that is sure to win the hearts of the children for whom it is intended."—*London Society.*

THE GREAT DUTCH ADMIRALS. By **Jacob de Liefde**. Crown 8vo. Illustrated. Price 5s.

"A really good book."—*Standard.*
"May be recommended as a wholesome present for boys. They will find in it numerous tales of adventure."—*Athenæum.*

"Thoroughly interesting and inspiriting."—*Public Opinion.*
"A really excellent book."—*Spectator.*

New Edition.

THE DESERT PASTOR, JEAN JAROUSSEAU. Translated from the French of **Eugene Pelletan**. By Colonel **E. P. De L'Hoste**. In fcap. 8vo, with an Engraved Frontispiece. Price 3s. 6d.

"There is a poetical simplicity and picturesqueness; the noblest heroism; unpretentious religion; pure love, and the spectacle of a household brought up in the fear of the Lord. . . . ."—*Illustrated London News.*

"This charming specimen of Eugène Pelletan's tender grace, humour, and hightoned morality."—*Notes and Queries.*
"A touching record of the struggles in the cause of religious liberty of a real man."—*Graphic.*

THE DESERTED SHIP. A Real Story of the Atlantic. By **Cupples Howe**, Master Mariner. Illustrated by **Townley Green**. Crown 8vo. 3s. 6d.

"Curious adventures with bears, seals, and other Arctic animals, and with scarcely more human Esquimaux, form the mass of

material with which the story deals, and will much interest boys who have a spice of romance in their composition."—*Courant.*

HOITY TOITY, THE GOOD LITTLE FELLOW. By **Charles Camden**. Illustrated. Crown 8vo. 3s. 6d.

"Young folks may gather a good deal of wisdom from the story, which is written in an amusing and attractive style."—*Courant.*
"Relates very pleasantly the history of

a charming little fellow who meddles always with a kindly disposition with other people's affairs and helps them to do right. There are many shrewd lessons to be picked up in this clever little story."—*Public Opinion.*

65, *Cornhill; & 12, Paternoster Row, London.*

Works Published by Henry S. King & Co.,

POETRY.

LYRICS OF LOVE FROM SHAKESPEARE TO TENNYSON. Selected and arranged by **W. Davenport Adams.** Fcap. 8vo, price 3s. 6d.

"*He has the prettiest love-songs for maids.*"—*Shakespeare.*
DEDICATED BY PERMISSION TO THE POET LAUREATE.

WILLIAM CULLEN BRYANT'S POEMS. Red-line Edition. Handsomely bound. With Illustrations and Portrait of the Author. Price 7s. 6d.

A Cheaper Edition is also published. Price 3s. 6d.

These are the only complete English Editions sanctioned by the Author.

ENGLISH SONNETS. Collected and Arranged by **John Dennis.** Small crown 8vo. Elegantly bound, price 3s. 6d.

HOME-SONGS FOR QUIET HOURS. By the **Rev. Canon R. H. Baynes**, Editor of "English Lyrics" and "Lyra Anglicana."

Handsomely printed and bound, price 3s. 6d.

THE DISCIPLES. A New Poem. By **Harriet Eleanor Hamilton King.** Crown 8vo. 7s. 6d.

The present work was commenced at the express instance of the great Italian patriot, Mazzini, and commemorates some of his associates and fellow-workers—men who looked up to him as their master and teacher. The author enjoyed the privilege of Mazzini's friendship, and the first part of this work was on its way to him when tidings reached this country that he had passed away.

SONGS FOR MUSIC. By **Four Friends.** Square crown 8vo.

CONTAINING SONGS BY
Reginald A. Gatty.   Stephen H. Gatty.
Greville J. Chester.   J. H. E.

THE POETICAL AND PROSE WORKS OF ROBERT BUCHANAN. A Collected Edition, in 5 Vols.

Vol. I. Contains—"Ballads and Romances;" "Ballads and Poems of Life."
Vol. II.—"Ballads and Poems of Life;"
"Allegories and Sonnets."
Vol. III.—"Cruiskeen Sonnets;" "Book of Orm;" "Political Mystics."

The Contents of the remaining Volumes will be duly announced.

THOUGHTS IN VERSE. Small crown 8vo.

This is a Collection of Verses expressive of religious feeling, written from a Theistic stand-point.

COSMOS. A Poem. Small crown 8vo.

SUBJECT.—Nature in the Past and in the Present.—Man in the Past and in the Present.—The Future.

VIGNETTES IN RHYME. Collected Verses. By **Austin Dobson.** Crown 8vo. Price 5s.

A Collection of Vers de Société, for the most part contributed to various magazines.

NARCISSUS AND OTHER POEMS. By **E. Carpenter.** Small crown 8vo. Price 5s.

A TALE OF THE SEA, SONNETS, AND OTHER POEMS. By **James Howell.** Crown 8vo, cloth, 5s.

IMITATIONS FROM THE GERMAN OF SPITTA AND TERSTEGEN. By **Lady Durand.** Crown 8vo. 4s.

"*An acceptable addition to the religious poetry of the day.*"—*Courant.*

METRICAL TRANSLATIONS FROM THE GREEK AND LATIN POETS, AND OTHER POEMS. By **R. B. Boswell, M.A.** Oxon. Crown 8vo.

65, Cornhill; & 12, Paternoster Row, London.

POETRY—*continued.*

ON VIOL AND FLUTE. A New Volume of Poems, by Edmund W. Gosse. With a Frontispiece by W. B. Scott. Crown 8vo.

EASTERN LEGENDS AND STORIES IN ENGLISH VERSE. By Lieutenant Norton Powlett, Royal Artillery. Crown 8vo. 5s.

"Have we at length found a successor to Thomas Ingoldsby? We are almost inclined to hope so after reading 'Eastern Legends.' There is a rollicking sense of fun about the stories, joined to marvellous power of rhyming, and plenty of swing, which irresistibly reminds us of our old favourite."—*Graphic.*

EDITH; OR, LOVE AND LIFE IN CHESHIRE. By T. Ashe, Author of the "Sorrows of Hypsipyle," etc. Sewed. Price 6d.

"A really fine poem, full of tender, subtle touches of feeling."—*Manchester News.*

"Pregnant from beginning to end with the results of careful observation and imaginative power."—*Chester Chronicle.*

THE GALLERY OF PIGEONS, AND OTHER POEMS. By Theo. Marzials. Crown 8vo. 4s. 6d.

"A conceit abounding in prettiness."—*Examiner.*

"Contains as clear evidence as a book can contain that its composition was a source of keen and legitimate enjoyment. The rush of fresh, sparkling fancies is too rapid, too sustained, too abundant, not to be spontaneous."—*Academy.*

THE INN OF STRANGE MEETINGS, AND OTHER POEMS. By Mortimer Collins. Crown 8vo. 5s.

"Abounding in quiet humour, in bright fancy, in sweetness and melody of expression, and, at times, in the tenderest touches of pathos."—*Graphic.*

"Mr. Collins has an undercurrent of chivalry and romance beneath the trifling vein of good-humoured banter which is the special characteristic of his verse."—*Athenæum.*

EROS AGONISTES. By E. B. D. Crown 8vo. 3s. 6d.

"The author of these verses has written a very touching story of the human heart in the story he tells with such pathos and power, of an affection cherished so long and so secretly. . . . It is not the least merit of these pages that they are everywhere illumined with moral and religious sentiment suggested, not paraded, of the brightest, purest character."—*Standard.*

CALDERON'S DRAMAS.
 THE PURGATORY OF ST. PATRICK.
 THE WONDERFUL MAGICIAN.
 LIFE IS A DREAM.
Translated from the Spanish. By Denis Florence MacCarthy. 10s.

These translations have never before been published. The "Purgatory of St. Patrick" is a new version, with new and elaborate historical notes.

SONGS FOR SAILORS. By Dr. W. C. Bennett. Dedicated by Special Request to H. R. H. the Duke of Edinburgh. Crown 8vo. 3s. 6d. With Steel Portrait and Illustrations.

An Edition in Illustrated paper Covers. Price 1s.

WALLED IN, AND OTHER POEMS. By the Rev. Henry J. Bulkeley. Crown 8vo. 5s.

"A remarkable book of genuine poetry."—*Evening Standard.*

"Genuine power displayed."—*Examiner.*

". . . . . Poetical feeling is manifest here, and the diction of the poem is unimpeachable."—*Pall Mall Gazette.*

"He has successfully attempted what has seldom before been well done, viz., the treatment of subjects not in themselves poetical from a poetic point of view."—*Graphic.*

"Intensity of feeling, a rugged pathos, robustness of tone, and a downrightness of expression which does not shrink from even slang if it seem best fitted for his purpose."—*Illustrated London News.*

SONGS OF LIFE AND DEATH. By John Payne, Author of "Intaglios," "Sonnets," "The Masque of Shadows," etc. Crown 8vo. 5s.

"The art of ballad-writing has long been lost in England, and Mr. Payne may claim to be its restorer. It is a perfect delight to meet with such a ballad as 'May Margaret' in the present volume."—*Westminster Review.*

ASPROMONTE, AND OTHER POEMS. Second Edition, cloth. 4s. 6d.

"The volume is anonymous, but there is no reason for the author to be ashamed of it. The 'Poems of Italy' are evidently inspired by genuine enthusiasm in the cause espoused, and one of them, 'The Execution of Felice Orsini,' has much poetic merit, the event celebrated being told with dramatic force."—*Athenæum.*

"The verse is fluent and free."—*Spectator.*

POETRY—*continued.*

A NEW VOLUME OF SONNETS. By the Rev. C. Tennyson Turner. Crown 8vo. 4s. 6d.

"Mr. Turner is a genuine poet; his song is sweet and pure, beautiful in expression, and often subtle in thought."—*Pall Mall Gazette.*

"The dominant charm of all these sonnets is the pervading presence of the writer's personality, never obtruded but always impalpably diffused. The light of a devout, gentle, and kindly spirit, a delicate and graceful fancy, a keen intelligence irradiates these thoughts."—*Contemporary Review.*

GOETHE'S FAUST. A New Translation in Rime. By the Rev. C. Kegan Paul. Crown 8vo. 6s.

"His translation is the most minutely accurate that has yet been produced..."—*Examiner.*

"Mr. Paul evidently understands 'Faust,' and his translation is as well suited to convey its meaning to English readers as any we have yet seen."—*Edinburgh Daily Review.*

"Mr. Paul is a zealous and a faithful interpreter."—*Saturday Review.*

THE DREAM AND THE DEED, AND OTHER POEMS. By Patrick Scott, Author of "Footpaths between Two Worlds," etc. Fcap. 8vo, cloth, 5s.

"A bitter and able satire on the vice and follies of the day, literary, social, and political."—*Standard.*

"Shows real poetic power coupled with evidences of satirical energy."—*Edinburgh Daily Review.*

SONGS OF TWO WORLDS. By a New Writer. Fcap. 8vo, cloth, 5s. Second Edition.

"These poems will assuredly take high rank among the class to which they belong."—*British Quarterly Review, April 1st.*

"If these poems are the mere preludes of a mind growing in power and in inclination for verse, we have in them the promise of a fine poet."—*Spectator, February 17th.*

"No extracts could do justice to the exquisite tones, the felicitous phrasing and delicately wrought harmonies of some of these poems."—*Nonconformist, March 27th.*

"It has a purity and delicacy of feeling like morning air."—*Graphic, March 16th.*

THE LEGENDS OF ST. PATRICK AND OTHER POEMS. By Aubrey de Vere. Crown 8vo. 5s.

"Mr. De Vere's versification in his earlier poems is characterised by great sweetness and simplicity. He is master of his instrument, and rarely offends the ear with false notes. Poems such as these scarcely admit of quotation, for their charm is not, and ought not to be, found in isolated passages; but we can promise the patient and thoughtful reader much pleasure in the perusal of this volume."—*Pall Mall Gazette.*

"We have marked, in almost every page, excellent touches from which we know not how to select. We have but space to commend the varied structure of his verse, the carefulness of his grammar, and his excellent English."—*Saturday Review.*

FICTION.

THE OWL'S NEST IN THE CITY. In 1 vol. Cloth, crown 8vo.

TWO GIRLS. By Frederick Wedmore, Author of "A Snapt Gold Ring." In 2 vols. Cloth, crown 8vo.

A powerful and dramatic story of Bohemian life in Paris and in London.

JUDITH GWYNNE. By Lisle Carr. In 3 vols. Crown 8vo, cloth.

MR. CARINGTON. A Tale of Love and Conspiracy. By Robert Turner Cotton. In 3 vols. Cloth, crown 8vo.

TOO LATE. By Mrs. Newman. Two vols. Crown 8vo.

A dramatic love story.

LADY MORETOUN'S DAUGHTER. By Mrs. Eiloart. In 3 vols. Crown 8vo, cloth.

FICTION—*continued.*

HEATHERGATE. In 2 vols. Cr. 8vo, cloth. A Story of Scottish Life and Character by a new Author.

THE QUEEN'S SHILLING. By **Captain Arthur Griffiths**, Author of " Peccavi." 2 vols.

". . . . A very lively and agreeable novel."—*Vanity Fair.*

"'The Queen's Shilling' is a capital story, far more interesting than the meagre sketch we have given of the fortunes of the hero and heroine can suggest. Every scene, character, and incident of the book are so life-like that they seem drawn from life direct."—*Pall Mall Gazette.*

MIRANDA. A Midsummer Madness. By **Mortimer Collins.** 3 vols.

"There is not a dull page in the whole three volumes."—*Standard.*

"The work of a man who is at once a thinker and a poet."—*Hour.*

SQUIRE SILCHESTER'S WHIM. By **Mortimer Collins**, Author of "Marquis and Merchant," "The Princess Clarice," &c. Crown 8vo. 3 vols.

"We think it the best (story) Mr. Collins has yet written. Full of incident and adventure."—*Pall Mall Gazette.*

"Decidedly the best novel from the pen of Mr. Mortimer Collins that we have yet come across."—*Graphic.*

"So clever, so irritating, and so charming a story."—*Standard.*

THE PRINCESS CLARICE. A Story of 1871. By **Mortimer Collins.** 2 vols. Crown 8vo.

"Mr. Collins has produced a readable book, amusingly characteristic. . . . ."—*Athenæum.*

"Very readable and amusing. We would especially give an honourable mention to Mr. Collins's '*vers de société*,' the writing of which has almost become a lost art."—*Pall Mall Gazette.*

"A bright, fresh, and original book."—*Standard.*

WHAT 'TIS TO LOVE. By the Author of "Flora Adair," "The Value of Fosterstown." 3 vols.

REGINALD BRAMBLE, A Cynic of the 19th Century. An Autobiography. One Volume.

"There is plenty of vivacity in Mr. Bramble's narrative."—*Athenæum.*

"Written in a lively and readable style."—*Hour.*

"The skill of the author in the delineation of the supposed chronicler, and the preservation of his natural character, is beyond praise."—*Morning Post.*

EFFIE'S GAME; How she Lost and How she Won. By **Cecil Clayton.** 2 vols.

"Well written. The characters move, and act, and, above all, talk like human beings, and we have liked reading about them."—*Spectator.*

CHESTERLEIGH. By **Ansley Conyers.** 3 vols. Crown 8vo.

"We have gained much enjoyment from the book."—*Spectator.*

"Will suit the hosts of readers of the higher class of romantic fiction."—*Morning Advertiser.*

BRESSANT. A Romance. By **Julian Hawthorne.** 2 vols. Crown 8vo.

"The son's work we venture to say is worthy of the sire. . . . The story as it stands is one of the most powerful with which we are acquainted."—*Times.*

"Pretty certain of meeting in this country a grateful and appreciative reception."—*Athenæum.*

"Mr. Julian Hawthorne is endowed with a large share of his father's peculiar genius."—*Pall Mall Gazette.*

"Enough to make us hopeful that we shall once more have reason to rejoice whenever we hear that a new work is coming out written by one who bears the honoured name of Hawthorne."—*Saturday Review.*

HONOR BLAKE: The Story of a Plain Woman. By **Mrs. Keatinge**, Author of "English Homes in India," &c. 2 vols. Crown 8vo.

"One of the best novels we have met with for some time."—*Morning Post.*

"A story which must do good to all, young and old, who read it."—*Daily News.*

65, *Cornhill;* & 12, *Paternoster Row, London.*

FICTION—continued.

OFF THE SKELLIGS. By Jean Ingelow. (Her First Romance.) Crown 8vo. In 4 vols.

"Clever and sparkling."—*Standard.*
"We read each succeeding volume with increasing interest, going almost to the point of wishing there was a fifth."—*Athenæum.*
"The novel as a whole is a remarkable one, because it is uncompromisingly true to life."—*Daily News.*

SEETA. By Colonel Meadows Taylor, Author of "Tara," "Ralph Darnell," &c. Crown 8vo. 3 vols.

"The story is well told, native life is admirably described, and the petty intrigues of native rulers, and their hatred of the English, mingled with fear lest the latter should eventually prove the victors, are cleverly depicted."—*Athenæum.*
"We cannot speak too highly of Colonel Meadows Taylor's book. . . . We would recommend all novel-readers to purchase it at the earliest opportunity."—*John Bull.*
"Thoroughly interesting and enjoyable reading."—*Examiner.*

HESTER MORLEY'S PROMISE. By Hesba Stretton. 3 vols.

"'Hester Morley's Promise' is much better than the average novel of the day; it has much more claim to critical consideration as a piece of literary work,—not mere mechanism. The pictures of a narrow society—narrow of soul and intellect—in which the book abounds, are very clever."—*Spectator.*
"Its charm lies not so much, perhaps, in any special excellence in character, drawing, or construction—though all the characters stand out clearly and are well sustained, and the interest of the story never flags—as in general tone and colouring."—*Observer.*

THE DOCTOR'S DILEMMA. By Hesba Stretton, Author of "Little Meg," &c., &c. Crown 8vo. 3 vols.

"A fascinating story which scarcely flags in interest from the first page to the last. It is all story; every page contributes something to the result."—*British Quarterly Review.*

THE ROMANTIC ANNALS OF A NAVAL FAMILY. By Mrs. Arthur Traherne. Crown 8vo. 10s. 6d.

"A very readable and interesting book."—*United Service Gazette,* June 28, 1873.
"Some interesting letters are introduced, amongst others, several from the late King William IV."—*Spectator.*
"Well and pleasantly told. There are also some capital descriptions of English country life in the last century, presenting a vivid picture of England before the introduction of railways, and the busy life accompanying them."—*Evening Standard.*

JOHANNES OLAF. By E. de Wille. Translated by F. E. Bunnett. Crown 8vo. 3 vols.

"The art of description is fully exhibited; perception of character and capacity for delineating it are obvious; while there is great breadth and comprehensiveness in the plan of the story."—*Morning Post.*

THE SPINSTERS OF BLATCHINGTON. By Mar. Travers. 2 vols. Crown 8vo.

"A pretty story. Deserving of a favourable reception."—*Graphic.*
"A book of more than average merits, worth reading."—*Examiner.*

A GOOD MATCH. By Amelia Perrier, Author of "Mea Culpa." 2 vols.

"Racy and lively."—*Athenæum.*
"As pleasant and readable a novel as we have seen this season."—*Examiner.*
"This clever and amusing novel."—*Pall Mall Gazette.*
"Agreeably written."—*Public Opinion.*

THOMASINA. By the Author of "Dorothy," "De Cressy," etc. 2 vols. Crown 8vo.

"A finished and delicate cabinet picture, no line is without its purpose, but all contribute to the unity of the work."—*Athenæum.*
"For the delicacies of character-drawing, for play of incident, and for finish of style, we must refer our readers to the story itself."—*Daily News.*
"This undeniably pleasing story."—*Pall Mall Gazette.*

VANESSA. By the Author of "Thomasina." 2 vols. Crown 8vo. [*Shortly.*

Works Published by Henry S. King & Co.,

FICTION—*continued.*

THE STORY OF SIR EDWARD'S WIFE. By Hamilton Marshall, Author of "For Very Life." 1 vol. Crown 8vo.

"A quiet graceful little story."—*Spectator.*

"There are many clever conceits in it. . . . Mr. Hamilton Marshall can tell a story closely and pleasantly."—*Pall Mall Gazette.*

LINKED AT LAST. By F. E. Bunnett. 1 vol. Crown 8vo.

"'Linked at Last' contains so much of pretty description, natural incident, and delicate portraiture, that the reader who once takes it up will not be inclined to relinquish it without concluding the volume."—*Morning Post.*

"A very charming story."—*John Bull.*

PERPLEXITY. By Sydney Mostyn. 3 vols. Crown 8vo.

"Shows much lucidity—much power of portraiture."—*Examiner.*

"Written with very considerable power, great cleverness, and sustained interest."—*Standard.*

"The literary workmanship is good, and the story forcibly and graphically told."—*Daily News.*

MEMOIRS OF MRS. LÆTITIA BOOTHBY. By William Clark Russell, Author of "The Book of Authors." Crown 8vo. 7s. 6d.

"Clever and ingenious."—*Saturday Review.*

"One of the most delightful books I have read for a very long while. Thoroughly entertaining from the first page to the last."—*Judy.*

"Very clever book."—*Guardian.*

CRUEL AS THE GRAVE. By the Countess Von Bothmer. 3 vols. Crown 8vo.

"*Jealousy is cruel as the Grave.*"

"An interesting, though somewhat tragic story."—*Athenæum.*

"An agreeable, unaffected, and eminently readable novel."—*Daily News.*

Thirty-Second Edition.

GINX'S BABY; HIS BIRTH AND OTHER MISFORTUNES. By Edward Jenkins. Crown 8vo. Price 2s.

Fourteenth Thousand.

LITTLE HODGE. A Christmas Country Carol. By Edward Jenkins, Author of "Ginx's Baby," &c. Illustrated. Crown 8vo. 5s.

A Cheap Edition in paper covers, price 1s.

"Wise and humorous, but yet most pathetic."—*Nonconformist.*

"The pathos of some of the passages is extremely touching."—*Manchester Examiner.*

Sixth Edition.

LORD BANTAM. By Edward Jenkins, Author of "Ginx's Baby." Crown 8vo. Price 2s.

LUCHMEE AND DILLOO. A Story of West Indian Life. By Edward Jenkins, Author of "Ginx's Baby," "Little Hodge," &c. Two vols. Demy 8vo. Illustrated. [*Preparing.*

HER TITLE OF HONOUR. By Holme Lee. Second Edition. 1 vol. Crown 8vo.

"When the interest of a pathetic story is united the value of a definite and high purpose."—*Spectator.*

"A most exquisitely written story."—*Literary Churchman.*

THE TASMANIAN LILY. By James Bonwick. Crown 8vo. Illustrated. Price 5s.

"The characters of the story are capitally conceived, and are full of those touches which give them a natural appearance."—*Public Opinion.*

"An interesting and useful work."—*Hour.*

MIKE HOWE, THE BUSHRANGER OF VAN DIEMEN'S LAND. By James Bonwick, Author of "The Tasmanian Lily," &c. Crown 8vo. With a Frontispiece.

65, *Cornhill;* & 12, *Paternoster Row, London.*

FICTION—*continued.*

Second Edition.

SEPTIMIUS. A Romance. By **Nathaniel Hawthorne**, Author of "The Scarlet Letter," "Transformation," &c. 1 vol. Crown 8vo, cloth, extra gilt. 9s.

> The *Athenæum* says that "the book is full of Hawthorne's most characteristic writing."
> "One of the best examples of Hawthorne's writing; every page is impressed with his peculiar view of thought, conveyed in his own familiar way."—*Post.*

PANDURANG HARI; OR, MEMOIRS OF A HINDOO. A Tale of Mahratta Life sixty years ago. With a Preface, by **Sir H. Bartle E. Frere, G.C.S.I.,** &c. 2 vols. Crown 8vo. Price 21s.

> "There is a quaintness and simplicity in the roguery of the hero that makes his life as attractive as that of Guzman d'Alfarache or Gil Blas, and so we advise our readers not to be dismayed at the length of Pandurang Hari, but to read it resolutely through. If they do this they cannot, we think, fail to be both amused and interested."—*Times.*

MADEMOISELLE JOSEPHINE'S FRIDAYS, and other Stories. By **Miss M. Betham Edwards**, Author of "Kitty," &c. [*Shortly.*

> A collection of Miss Edwards' more important contributions to periodical literature.

Second Edition.

HERMANN AGHA. An Eastern Narrative. By **W. Gifford Palgrave**, Author of "Travels in Central Arabia," &c. 2 vols. Crown 8vo, cloth, extra gilt. 18s.

> "Reads like a tale of life, with all its incidents. The young will take to it for its love portions, the older for its descriptions, some in this day for its Arab philosophy."—*Athenæum.*
> "There is a positive fragrance as of newly-mown hay about it, as compared with the artificially perfumed passions which are detailed to us with such gusto by our ordinary novel-writers in their endless volumes."—*Observer.*

MARGARET AND ELIZABETH. A Story of the Sea. By **Katherine Saunders**, Author of "Gideon's Rock," &c. In 1 vol. Cloth, crown 8vo.

GIDEON'S ROCK, and other Stories. By **Katherine Saunders**. In one vol. Crown 8vo.

> CONTENTS.—Gideon's Rock.—Old Matthew's Puzzle.—Gentle Jack.—Uncle Ned.—The Retired Apothecary.

JOAN MERRYWEATHER, and other Stories. By **Katherine Saunders**. In one vol. Crown 8vo.

> CONTENTS.—The Haunted Crust.—The Flower-Girl—Joan Merryweather.—The Watchman's Story.—An Old Letter.

A New and Cheaper Edition, in 1 vol. each, Illustrated, price 6s., of

COL. MEADOWS TAYLOR'S INDIAN TALES is preparing for publication. The First Volume will be "The Confessions of a Thug," and will be published in December, to be followed by "Tara," "Ralph Darnell," "Tippoo Sultan."

THEOLOGICAL.

STUDIES IN MODERN PROBLEMS. A Series of Essays by various Writers. Edited by the **Rev. Orby Shipley, M.A.**

This project secures the supervision of a small number of Clergy and Laity formed of representative men in London, at both Universities, and in the Provinces, who have promised their co-operation editorially, and will act as a Committee of Reference. The first issue will consist of a series of 12 or 13 Tractates, by various writers, of 48 pages each, in a readable type, crown 8vo, at the price of 6*d*., and will appear fortnightly for six months, by way of trial.

A Single Copy sent post free for 7*d*.
The Series of 12 Numbers sent post free for 7*s*., or for 7*s*. 6*d*. if 13 } *if prepaid*.
Additional Copies sent at proportionate rates.

PROPOSED SUBJECTS AND AUTHORS.
(AMONGST OTHERS:)

SACRAMENTAL CONFESSION.
    A. H. WARD, M.A.
RETREATS FOR PERSONS LIVING IN THE WORLD.
    T. T. CARTER, M.A.
ABOLITION OF THE ARTICLES.
    NICHOLAS POCOCK, M.A.
CREATION AND MODERN SCIENCE.
    GEORGE GREENWOOD, M.A.
MISSIONS. J. EDWARD VAUX, M.A.
CATHOLIC AND PROTESTANT.
    EDWARD L. BLENKINSOPP, M.A.

SOME PRINCIPLES OF CEREMONIAL. J. E. FIELD, M.A.
THE SANCTITY OF MARRIAGE.
    JOHN WALTER LEA, B.A.
RESERVATION OF THE BLESSED SACRAMENT.
    HENRY HUMBLE, M.A.
CATHOLICISM AND PROGRESS.
    EDMUND G. WOOD, M.A.
A LAYMAN'S VIEW OF CONFESSION.
    J. DAVID CHAMBERS, M.A.

UNTIL THE DAY DAWN. Four Advent Lectures delivered in the Episcopal Chapel, Milverton, Warwickshire, on the Sunday evenings during Advent, 1870. By the **Rev. Marmaduke E. Browne.** Crown 8vo.

A SCOTCH COMMUNION SUNDAY. To which are added Certain Discourses from a University City. By **A. K. H. B.**, Author of "The Recreations of a Country Parson." Crown 8vo. Price 5*s*.

CHURCH THOUGHT AND CHURCH WORK. Edited by the **Rev. Chas. Anderson, M.A.**, Editor of "Words and Works in a London Parish." Demy 8vo. Pp. 250. 7*s*. 6*d*. Containing Articles by the Rev. J. LL. DAVIES, J. M. CAPES, HARRY JONES, BROOKE LAMBERT, A. J. ROSS, Professor CHEETHAM, the EDITOR, and others.

WORDS AND WORKS IN A LONDON PARISH. Edited by the **Rev. Charles Anderson, M.A.** Demy 8vo. 6*s*.

"It has an interest of its own for not a few minds, to whom the question 'Is the National Church worth preserving as such, and if so how best increase its vital power?' is of deep and grave importance."—*Spectator*.

EVERY DAY A PORTION: Adapted from the Bible and the Prayer Book, for the Private Devotions of those living in Widowhood. Collected and Edited by the **Lady Mary Vyner.** Square crown 8vo, printed on good paper, elegantly bound.

"Now she that is a widow indeed, and desolate, trusteth in God."

THEOLOGICAL—*continued.*

WORDS OF HOPE FROM THE PULPIT OF THE TEMPLE CHURCH. By C. J. Vaughan, D.D., Master of the Temple.

Third Edition.

THE YOUNG LIFE EQUIPPING ITSELF FOR GOD'S SERVICE. Being Four Sermons Preached before the University of Cambridge in November, 1872. By the **Rev. C. J. Vaughan, D.D.**, Master of the Temple. Crown 8vo. Price 3s. 6d.

"Has all the writer's characteristics of devotedness, purity, and high moral tone."—*London Quarterly Review.*
"As earnest, eloquent, and as liberal as everything else that he writes."—*Examiner.*
"Earnest in tone and eloquent in entreaty."—*Manchester Examiner.*

A NEW VOLUME OF ACADEMIA ESSAYS. Edited by the Most Reverend Archbishop Manning. Demy.

CONTENTS:—The Philosophy of Christianity.—Mystical Elements of Religion.—Controversy with the Agnostics.—A Reasoning Thought.—Darwinism brought to Book.—Mr. Mill on Liberty of the Press.—Christianity in relation to Society.—The Religious Condition of Germany.—The Philosophy of Bacon.—Catholic Laymen and Scholastic Philosophy.

WHY AM I A CHRISTIAN? By **Viscount Stratford de Redcliffe**, P.C., K.G., G.C.B. Crown 8vo. 3s. Third Edition.

"Has a peculiar interest, as exhibiting the convictions of an earnest, intelligent, and practical man."—*Contemporary Review.*

THEOLOGY AND MORALITY. Being Essays by the **Rev. J. Llewellyn Davies.** 1 vol. 8vo. Price 7s. 6d.

Essays on Questions of Belief and Practice.—The Debts of Theology to Secular Influences.—The Christian Theory of Duty.—Weak Points in Utilitarianism.—Nature and Prayer.—The Continuity of Creation.—The Beginnings of the Church.—Erastus and Excommunication.—Pauperism as produced by Wealth.—Combinations of Agricultural Labourers.—Communism.

"There is a good deal that is well worth reading."—*Church Times.*

THE RECONCILIATION OF RELIGION AND SCIENCE. Being Essays by the **Rev. T. W. Fowle, M.A.** 1 vol., 8vo. 10s. 6d.

The Divine Character of Christ.—Science and Immortality.—Morality and Immortality.—Christianity and Immortality.—Religion and Fact.—The Miracles of God.—The Miracles of Man.—A Scientific Account of Inspiration.—The Inspiration of the Jews.—The Inspiration of the Bible.—The Divinity of Christ and Modern Thought.—The Church and the Working Classes.

"A book which requires and deserves the respectful attention of all reflecting Churchmen. It is earnest, reverent, thoughtful, and courageous . . . There is scarcely a page in the book which is not equally worthy of a thoughtful pause."—*Literary Churchman.*

HYMNS AND VERSES, Original and Translated. By the **Rev. Henry Downton.** Small crown 8vo, 3s. 6d.

"It is a rare gift and very precious, and we heartily commend this, as fruits, to the pious in all denominations."—*Church Opinion.*
"Considerable force and beauty characterise some of these verses."—*Watchman.*
"Mr. Downton's 'Hymns and Verses' are worthy of all praise."—*English Churchman.*
"Will, we do not doubt, be welcome as a permanent possession to those for whom they have been composed or to whom they have been originally addressed."—*Church Herald.*

Works Published by Henry S. King & Co., 33

THEOLOGICAL—*continued.*

MISSIONARY ENTERPRISE IN THE EAST. By the **Rev. Richard Collins.** Illustrated. Crown 8vo. 6s.

"A very graphic story told in lucid, simple, and modest style."—*English Churchman.*

"A readable and very interesting volume."—*Church Review.*

"It is a real pleasure to read an honest book on Missionary work, every word of which shows the writer to be a man of large heart, far-seeing views, and liberal cultivation, and such a book we have now before us."—*Mission Life.*

"We may judge from our own experience, no one who takes up this charming little volume will lay it down again till he has got to the last word."—*John Bull.*

THE ETERNAL LIFE. Being Fourteen Sermons. By the **Rev. Jas. Noble Bennie, M.A.** Crown 8vo. 6s.

"We recommend these sermons as wholesome Sunday reading."—*English Churchman.*

"Very chaste and pure in style."—*Courant.*

"The whole volume is replete with matter for thought and study."—*John Bull.*

"Mr. Bennie preaches earnestly and well."—*Literary Churchman.*

THE REALM OF TRUTH. By **Miss E. T. Carne.** Crown 8vo. 5s. 6d.

"A singularly calm, thoughtful, and philosophical inquiry into what Truth is, and what its authority."—*Leeds Mercury.*

"It tells the world what it does not like to hear, but what it cannot be told too often, that Truth is something stronger and more enduring than our little doings, and speakings, and actings."—*Literary Churchman.*

LIFE: Conferences delivered at Toulouse. By the **Rev. Père Lacordaire.** Crown 8vo. 6s.

"Let the serious reader cast his eye upon any single page in this volume, and he will find there words which will arrest his attention and give him a desire to know more of the teachings of this worthy follower of the saintly St. Dominick."—*Morning Post.*

"The book is worth studying as an evidence of the way in which an able man may be crippled by theological chains."—*Examiner.*

"The discourses are simple, natural, and unaffectedly eloquent."—*Public Opinion.*

Fourth Edition.

THOUGHTS FOR THE TIMES. By the **Rev. H. R. Haweis, M.A.,** "Author of Music and Morals," etc. Crown 8vo. 7s. 6d.

"Bears marks of much originality of thought and individuality of expression."—*Pall Mall Gazette.*

"Mr. Haweis writes not only fearlessly, but with remarkable freshness and vigour. In all that he says we perceive a transparent honesty and singleness of purpose."—*Saturday Review.*

SPEECH IN SEASON. A New Volume of Sermons. By the **Rev. H. R. Haweis.** [*Preparing.*

Second Edition.

CATHOLICISM AND THE VATICAN. With a Narrative of the Old Catholic Congress at Munich. By **J. Lowry Whittle, A.M.,** Trin. Coll., Dublin. Crown 8vo. 4s. 6d.

"We may cordially recommend his book to all who wish to follow the course of the Old Catholic movement."—*Saturday Review.*

65, *Cornhill;* & 12, *Paternoster Row, London.*

THEOLOGICAL—*continued*.

Second Edition.

SCRIPTURE LANDS IN CONNECTION WITH THEIR HISTORY. By **G. S. Drew, M.A.**, Vicar of Trinity, Lambeth, Author of "Reasons of Faith." Bevelled boards, 8vo. Price 10s. 6d.

"Mr. Drew has invented a new method of illustrating Scripture history—from observation of the countries. Instead of narrating his travels, and referring from time to time to the facts of sacred history belonging to the different countries, he writes an outline history of the Hebrew nation from Abraham downwards, with special reference to the various points in which the geography illustrates the history. . . . He is very successful in picturing to his readers the scenes before his own mind."—*Saturday Review*.

Second Edition.

NAZARETH: ITS LIFE AND LESSONS. By the **Rev. G. S. Drew**, Vicar of Trinity, Lambeth. Second Edition. In small 8vo, cloth. 5s.

"A singularly reverent and beautiful book."—*Daily Telegraph*.
"Perhaps one of the most remarkable books recently issued in the whole range of English theology."—*Churchman's Magazine*.

THE DIVINE KINGDOM ON EARTH AS IT IS IN HEAVEN. By the **Rev. G. S. Drew**, Author of "Nazareth: its Life and Lessons." In demy 8vo, bound in cloth. Price 10s. 6d.

"Thoughtful and eloquent. . . . Full of original thinking admirably expressed."—*British Quarterly Review*.
"Entirely valuable and satisfactory."
". . . . There is no living divine to whom the authorship would not be a credit."—*Literary Churchman*.

SIX PRIVY COUNCIL JUDGMENTS—1850-1872. Annotated by **W. G. Brooke, M.A.**, Barrister-at-Law. Crown 8vo. 9s.

THE MOST COMPLETE HYMN BOOK PUBLISHED.

HYMNS FOR THE CHURCH AND HOME. Selected and Edited by the **Rev. W. Fleming Stevenson**, Author of "Praying and Working."

The Hymn-book consists of Three Parts:—I. For Public Worship.—II. For Family and Private Worship.—III. For Children: and contains Biographical Notices of nearly 300 Hymn-writers, with Notes upon their Hymns.

*_{*} Published in various forms and prices, the latter ranging from 8d. to 6s. Lists and full particulars will be furnished on application to the Publisher.

WORKS OF THE LATE REV. F. W. ROBERTSON.

NEW AND CHEAPER EDITIONS.

SERMONS.
    Vol. I. Small crown 8vo. Price 3s. 6d.
     ,, II. Small crown 8vo. Price 3s. 6d.
     ,, III. Small crown 8vo. Price 3s. 6d.
     ,, IV. Small crown 8vo. Price 3s. 6d.

EXPOSITORY LECTURES ON ST. PAUL'S EPISTLE TO THE CORINTHIANS. Small crown 8vo. 5s.

AN ANALYSIS OF MR. TENNYSON'S "IN MEMORIAM." (Dedicated by permission to the Poet-Laureate.) Fcap. 8vo. 2s.

WORKS OF THE LATE REV. F. W. ROBERTSON—*continued*.

THE EDUCATION OF THE HUMAN RACE. Translated from the German of **Gotthold Ephraim Lessing**. Fcap. 8vo. 2s. 6d.

LECTURES AND ADDRESSES, WITH OTHER LITERARY REMAINS. By the late **Rev. Fredk. W. Robertson**. A New Edition, including a Correspondence with Lady Byron. With Introduction by the **Rev. Stopford A. Brooke, M.A.** In One Vol. Uniform with the Sermons. Price 5s. [*Preparing*.

A LECTURE ON FRED. W. ROBERTSON, M.A. By the **Rev. F. A. Noble**, delivered before the Young Men's Christian Association of Pittsburgh, U.S. 1s. 6d.

WORKS BY THE REV. STOPFORD A. BROOKE, M.A.
Chaplain in Ordinary to Her Majesty the Queen.

THE LATE REV. F. W. ROBERTSON, M.A., LIFE AND LETTERS OF. Edited by **Stopford Brooke, M.A.**, Chaplain in Ordinary to the Queen.

In 2 vols., uniform with the Sermons. Price 7s. 6d.
Library Edition, in demy 8vo, with Two Steel Portraits. 12s.
A Popular Edition, in 1 vol. Price 6s.

THEOLOGY IN THE ENGLISH POETS. Being Lectures delivered by the **Rev. Stopford A. Brooke**, Chaplain in Ordinary to Her Majesty the Queen.

Third Edition.

CHRIST IN MODERN LIFE. Sermons Preached in St. James's Chapel, York Street, London. Crown 8vo. 7s. 6d.

"Nobly fearless and singularly strong. . . . carries our admiration throughout."
—*British Quarterly Review*.

Second Edition.

FREEDOM IN THE CHURCH OF ENGLAND. Six Sermons suggested by the Voysey Judgment. In 1 vol. Crown 8vo, cloth. 3s. 6d.

"A very fair statement of the views in respect to freedom of thought held by the liberal party in the Church of England."—*Blackwood's Magazine*.

"Interesting and readable, and characterised by great clearness of thought, frankness of statement, and moderation of tone."—*Church Opinion*.

Seventh Edition.

SERMONS Preached in St. James's Chapel, York Street, London. Crown 8vo. 6s.

"No one who reads these sermons will wonder that Mr. Brooke is a great power in London, that his chapel is thronged, and his followers large and enthusiastic.

"They are fiery, energetic, impetuous sermons, rich with the treasures of a cultivated imagination."—*Guardian*.

THE LIFE AND WORK OF FREDERICK DENISON MAURICE: A Memorial Sermon. Crown 8vo, sewed. 1s.

65, *Cornhill;* & 12, *Paternoster Row, London.*

THE CORNHILL LIBRARY OF FICTION.

3s. 6d. per Volume.

IT is intended in this Series to produce books of such merit that readers will care to preserve them on their shelves. They are well printed on good paper, handsomely bound, with a Frontispiece, and are sold at the moderate price of 3s. 6d. each.

FOR LACK OF GOLD. By **Charles Gibbon.**

GOD'S PROVIDENCE HOUSE. By **Mrs. G. L. Banks.**

ROBIN GRAY. By **Charles Gibbon.** With a Frontispiece by **Hennessy.**

KITTY. By **Miss M. Betham-Edwards.**

READY MONEY MORTIBOY. A Matter-of-Fact Story.

HIRELL. By **John Saunders,** Author of "Abel Drake's Wife."

ONE OF TWO. By **J. Hain Friswell,** Author of "The Gentle Life," etc.

ABEL DRAKE'S WIFE. By **John Saunders.**

THE HOUSE OF RABY. By **Mrs. G. Hooper.**

A FIGHT FOR LIFE. By **Moy Thomas.**

OTHER STANDARD NOVELS TO FOLLOW.

65, *Cornhill;* and 12, *Paternoster Row,* London.

LIST OF AUTHORS, AND SUBJECTS OF THEIR BOOKS,

TO BE PUBLISHED IN THE

INTERNATIONAL SCIENTIFIC SERIES.

Prof. J. P. COOKE.
The New Chemistry.

Rev. M. J. BERKELEY, M.A. F.L.S. and M. COOKE, M.A. LL.D.
Fungi; their Nature, Influences, and Uses.

Prof. OSCAR SCHMIDT. (University of Strasburg.)
The Theory of Descent and Darwinism.

Prof. SHELDON AMOS.
The Science of Law.

Prof. VOGEL. (Polytechnic Academy of Berlin.)
The Chemical Effects of Light.

Prof. W. KINGDON CLIFFORD, M.A.
The First Principles of the Exact Sciences explained to the non-mathematical.

Prof. T. H. HUXLEY, LL.D. F.R.S.
Bodily Motion and Consciousness.

Dr. W. B. CARPENTER, LL.D. F.R.S.
The Physical Geography of the Sea.

Prof. WILLIAM ODLING, F.R.S.
The Old Chemistry from the new standpoint.

W. LAUDER LINDSAY, M.D. F.R.S.E.
Mind in the Lower Animals.

Sir JOHN LUBBOCK, Bart. F.R.S.
The Antiquity of Man.

Prof. W. T. THISELTON DYER, B.A. B.SC.
Form and Habit in Flowering Plants.

Mr. J. N. LOCKYER, F.R.S.
Spectrum Analysis.

Prof. MICHAEL FOSTER, M.D.
Protoplasm and the Cell Theory.

Prof. W. STANLEY JEVONS.
The Logic of Statistics.

Dr. H. CHARLTON BASTIAN, M.D. F.R.S.
The Brain as an Organ of Mind.

Prof. A. C. RAMSAY, LL.D. F.R.S.
Earth Sculpture: Hills, Valleys, Mountains, Plains, Rivers, Lakes; how they were Produced, and how they have been Destroyed.

Prof. RUDOLPH VIRCHOW. (University of Berlin.)
Morbid Physiological Action.

Prof. CLAUDE BERNARD. (College of France.)
Physical and Metaphysical Phenomena of Life.

Prof. A. QUETELET. (Brussels Acad. of Sciences.)
Social Physics.

Prof. H. SAINTE-CLAIRE DEVILLE.
An Introduction to General Chemistry.

Prof. WURTZ.
Atoms and the Atomic Theory.

Prof. DE QUATREFAGES.
The Negro Races.

Prof. LACAZE-DUTHIERS.
Zoology since Cuvier.

Prof. BERTHELOT.
Chemical Synthesis.

Prof. J. ROSENTHAL.
General Physiology of Muscles and Nerves.

Prof. JAMES D. DANA, M.A. LL.D.
On Cephalization; or, Head-Characters in the Gradation and Progress of Life.

Prof. S. W. JOHNSON, M.A.
On the Nutrition of Plants.

Prof. AUSTIN FLINT, Jr. M.D.
The Nervous System and its Relation to the Bodily Functions.

Prof. W. D. WHITNEY.
Modern Linguistic Science.

Prof. BERNSTEIN. (University of Halle.)
Physiology of the Senses.

Prof. FERDINAND COHN. (University of Breslau.)
Thallophytes (Algae Lichens Fungi).

Prof. HERMANN. (University of Zurich.)
Respiration.

Prof. LEUCKART. (University of Leipsic.)
Outlines of Animal Organization.

Prof. LIEBREICH. (University of Berlin.)
Outlines of Toxicology.

Prof. KUNDT. (University of Strasburg.)
On Sound.

Prof. LOMMEL. (University of Erlangen.)
Optics.

Prof. REES. (University of Erlangen.)
On Parasitic Plants.

Prof. STEINTHAL. (University of Berlin.)
Outlines of the Science of Language.

For LIST OF BOOKS ALREADY PUBLISHED see the beginning of the book.

HENRY S. KING & CO., 65 CORNHILL, AND 12 PATERNOSTER ROW, LONDON.

www.ingramcontent.com/pod-product-compliance
Lightning Source LLC
Chambersburg PA
CBHW021806230426
43669CB00008B/652